I0814853
19e
18e
METRO
9e
10e
2e
3e
4e
11e
20e
5e
M
12e
13e

THE EATER GUIDE TO Paris

Written by Lindsey Tramuta

Edited by Stephanie Wu

Illustrations by Alice Des

Abrams, New York

CONTENTS

INTRODUCTION

Paris is a city that never rests, at least when it comes to the national pastime of dining out—it's constantly finding ways to innovate, experiment, and, most importantly, have fun. There is no other destination where daily life so proudly revolves around food, where it's nearly impossible to have a bad meal, and where even humble supermarkets and green markets are culinary havens. Done right, visiting Paris can be a crash course in global food history, and a trip where street food, cozy bistro staples, and Michelin-starred restaurants get equal billing.

This guidebook is the natural evolution of Eater's award-winning coverage of, and deep love for, Paris. Eater began as a restaurant site in 2005, fervently covering the openings, closings, and power players of New York's dining scene. We eventually expanded to Los Angeles, San Francisco, and Chicago, and have, in the two decades since, evolved into a network covering more than twenty US cities, with countless guides to international culinary destinations.

Whether at home or abroad, our expertise has always been rooted in local authority, with contributors who understand firsthand how restaurants can define a city's culture and economy. At Eater, covering restaurants isn't just about food or hospitality, it's also the chronicling of food trends, of small business policy, of entrepreneurship, of dining habits, and even of the economy at large.

This book aims to capture the spirit of the city and its devotion to food. We've split the twenty arrondissements into seven sections, starting with the highly frequented Paris Centre (home to the Marais, the Jardin des Tuileries, and the Palais Royal) and Saint-Germain-des-Prés. For those who are willing to venture a little farther afield, we tackle the artsier and more diverse dining neighborhoods of Oberkampf, Chinatown, and Belleville. In each chapter, we've highlighted our absolute favorite restaurants and shops, ranging from iconic classics to intriguing newcomers. Paris is about so much more than French food, which is why we have dedicated explorations of Southeast Asian, Levantine, and West African cuisines—and the chefs and restaurateurs that have put an only-in-Paris spin on the food they grew up with. We have weekend itineraries to Champagne, Brittany, and Aix-en-Provence, because as much as Paris is chock-full of incredible food, it only scratches the surface of what the rest of France has to offer. And we have the need-to-know intel about dining etiquette, the best hotels to stay in, and how to nab the hottest tables.

Paris is one of the world's most-visited cities for good reason, but there's so much more to it than how it's portrayed in television and movies. We hope this book gives you a glimpse of the Paris that its residents love so deeply, where every trip uncovers a million more reasons to go back.

—**Stephanie Wu**, editor in chief

PRO TIP: Navigating Paris's arrondissements (or neighborhoods) can be tricky. To find your way around the city, remember that the arrondissements are numbered starting in the middle of the city, going clockwise and expanding out. And when looking at a restaurant's address, the final digits of the postal code will tell you which arrondissement it's in.

In addition to this book, two things can help you navigate: **Eater's regularly updated map of the city's essential restaurants** and **our ongoing coverage of this special destination.**

ESSENTIAL RESTAURANTS

EATER'S GUIDE TO PARIS

Les Halles
Louvre
Marais
North Marais
Palais Royal
Sentier

1st, 2nd,
ARRONDI

3rd, 4th

SSEMENTS

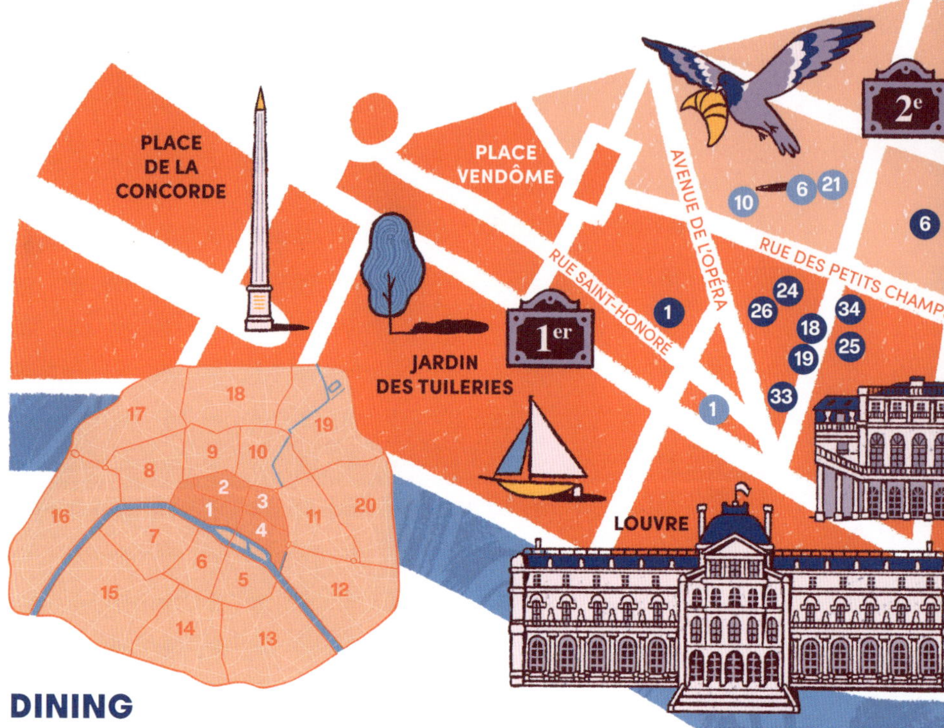

DINING

1 19 Saint Roch
2 L'As du Fallafel
3 Benoit
4 Bistrot des Tournelles
5 Bouillon République
6 La Bourse et La Vie
7 Breizh Café
8 The Cambridge Public House
9 Candelaria
10 Chez Alain Miam Miam
11 Chez l'Ami Louis
12 Chez Denise
13 Datil
14 Les Enfants du Marché
15 Frenchie Bar à Vins
16 Guefen
17 La Halle aux Grains
18 Juveniles
19 Kunitoraya
20 Liza
21 Mama Nissa
22 Mắm from Hanoï
23 Le Mary Celeste
24 Menkicchi Ramen
25 Nhome
26 On the Bab
27 Parcelles
28 La Poule au Pot
29 Racines
30 Restaurant Omar Dhiab
31 Shabour
32 Song Heng
33 Takara
34 Verjus
35 Yam'Tcha

SHOPPING

1 Astier de Villatte
2 Aux Merveilleux de Fred
3 Christophe Louie
4 E. Dehillerin
5 Épicerie du Marais
6 Épices Roellinger
7 Fou de Pâtisserie
8 G. Detou
9 Izraël
10 Kioko
11 Legrand Filles et Fils
12 Librairie Gourmande
13 Maison Aleph
14 Maison Plisson

1st, 2nd, 3rd, 4th ARRONDISSEMENTS

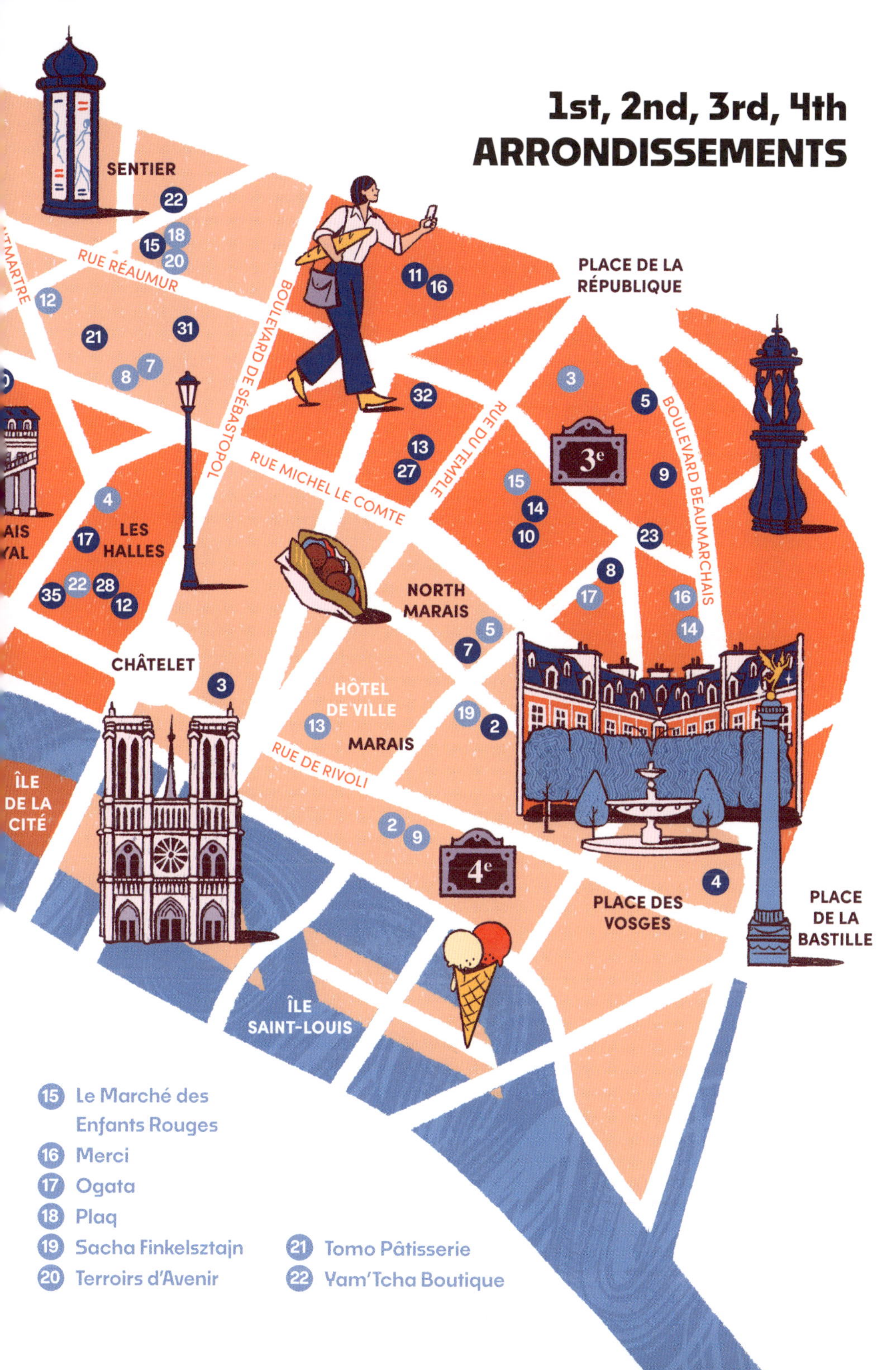

15 Le Marché des Enfants Rouges
16 Merci
17 Ogata
18 Plaq
19 Sacha Finkelsztajn
20 Terroirs d'Avenir
21 Tomo Pâtisserie
22 Yam'Tcha Boutique

1st, 2nd, 3rd, 4th ARRONDISSEMENTS DINING

Long before the 1st, 2nd, 3rd, and 4th arrondissements were administratively intertwined to form the Paris Centre district, they were already central in everything from business to dining and culture. If you imagine the snail-shaped layout of Paris, the 1st arrondissement sits at the city's very core, with the Louvre—the planet's largest museum—as its marquee destination abutting the Seine river. Vestiges of this area's 800-year reign as "the Belly of Paris," as Zola so famously nicknamed Les Halles market (see A Brief History of Dining in Paris), are omnipresent in the form of cafés, brasseries, and specialty shops.

The 1st arrondissement may be associated primarily with shopping, art, and cultural history, but it's full of exciting restaurants that should not be missed. Tucked behind the narrow streets of the seventeenth-century Palais Royal, with its manicured trees and the popular sculpture by Daniel Buren in the Courtyard of Honor, are some very special bistros and restaurants run by both international and

French chefs. Above the park, to the north, you'll land on rue Sainte-Anne, part of a neighborhood nicknamed Little Tokyo for its concentration of noodle shops, bakeries, and sushi bars—now also home to a rising crop of Korean restaurants.

Hook a left to the west, dipping in and out of some of the charming covered passages such as Galerie Colbert and Galerie Vivienne, and you're in the ritziest part of town—literally—at place Vendôme, home of the Ritz Paris and its famed Hemingway Bar. Originally completed in the 1700s for the city's wealthiest bankers, the mansions surrounding this square are now home to luxury jewelry, watch, and fashion boutiques. And mere blocks away, you'll find the Jardin des Tuileries, the oldest public garden in Paris.

Connecting Les Halles to the Sentier district (the one-time wholesale textile hub is now a food and tech center), the 2nd arrondissement's rue Montorgueil is a pedestrian thoroughfare occupied by specialty pastry, chocolate, tea, and other family-run boutiques, many of which date back centuries.

Traversing rue de Renard, which runs north/south, leads to the famed Marais, which covers both the 3rd and 4th arrondissements. From there, cross any number of the bridges along this part of the quai to discover Paris's two islands: Île de la Cité and Île Saint-Louis. On the former, you'll find the Conciergerie museum, where Marie Antoinette was jailed and beheaded, the stunning Sainte-Chapelle gothic chapel, and, of course, Notre-Dame; the latter is known for its quaint and quiet corners housing famous residents and businesses such as Berthillon, the city's best-known artisanal ice cream parlor.

Back on the mainland, the narrow rue des Rosiers and surrounding streets of the old Jewish quarter reveal a mix of competing falafel vendors and kosher delis. The Marais neighborhood and its narrow streets have long been the bastion of Jewish life. While there were Ashkenazi and Sephardic Jews in Paris through the Middle Ages until expulsion in 1394, it wasn't until the early 1880s up through the late 1930s that the diaspora expanded massively. More than 100,000 Yiddish-speaking Jews from Central and Eastern Europe fled the pogroms and arrived in France, settling mostly in the little pocket of the Marais nicknamed the Pletzl, Yiddish for "little square."

The further north you go, past the place des Vosges, which was initially built for socializing aristocrats, the more residential the Marais gets—especially around the rue de Bretagne, which is also home to the Marché des Enfants Rouges, the city's oldest covered market. Today, it's probably the closest Paris will get to an indoor food hall, with a mix of vendors selling produce, cheese, and meats for at-home cooking, and others offering prepared food to be eaten standing up at counters, at shared picnic tables, or inside trendy restaurants.

1. 19 Saint Roch

19, rue Saint-Roch, 75001

After making waves cooking at Aux Deux Amis, Vivant Deux, and Déviant, the young chef Pierre Touitou brought his apron on the road, cooking in Arles as a chef-in-residence. But in spring 2024, he returned to his Parisian roots and opened his first restaurant a few blocks from the Palais Royal. Much like his cooking, the restaurant is slick but pared back, big on retro style with only a few design components—black and white tiles and leather banquettes and mahogany wood furnishings. On the plate, that translates to no more than a few key ingredients or condiments at once. The menu is short and seasonal, but you might see lo bak go, a Chinese turnip cake that Touitou prepares like panisses (chickpea fritters); braised beef shoulder served with a side of pkaïla (stewed spinach) blended with beef tongue; and a boozy Black Forest cake for dessert.

2. L'As du Fallafel

34, rue des Rosiers, 75004

"Always imitated, never equaled," boasts the sign atop this rue des Rosiers falafel stalwart. Is it the best? That's a matter of personal preference, but to the aspirants who stand in lines that snake along the cobblestone street, the pita sandwiches overflowing with garlicky chickpea mounds, creamy hummus, lightly pickled red cabbage, fried eggplant, and topped with harissa, are more than worth the wait. Closed on Saturday for Shabbat.

3. Benoit

20, rue Saint-Martin, 75004

It's hard to get more nostalgic than this early twentieth-century bistro (shown above) with its wood paneling, brass light fixtures, stucco columns, and jovial waiters, run by Alain Ducasse—France's most famous chef and serial restaurateur—since 2005. The emphasis on classics is clear from the menu of lightly updated renditions of well-known dishes like pâté en croûte and escargot, blood sausage and sweetbreads, tête de veau, and cassoulet, with profiteroles and Savarin à l'Armagnac to finish. Expect appearances from Ducasse's own high-quality bean-to-bar chocolate, cookies, ice creams, and specialty coffees.

4. Bistrot des Tournelles

6, rue des Tournelles, 75004

Meat lovers book several weeks ahead for this revival bistro near the place de la Bastille, which gently encourages early diners to wrap up on time to accommodate a second seating. It's worth it for restaurateur Édouard Vermynck and chef Geoffroy Langella's supremely executed favorites served by candlelight. The grilled andouillette (tripe sausage) and filet de boeuf come with a bottomless plate of perfectly crisp fries, which go well with the Beaujolais-forward wine selection.

5. Bouillon République

39, boulevard du Temple, 75003

After Bouillon Pigalle made the bouillon format cool again (see page 64), this massive follow-up created a lively destination just off the place de la République. With nearly 450 seats spanning two floors, Bouillon République does filling, feel-good dishes like oeufs mayonnaise, veal blanquette, and boeuf bourguignon for a multigenerational crowd, at inconceivably gentle prices that extend to wine. Take advantage of the drink menu, too: everything from wine to soda is offered by the glass, bottle, magnum, and even jeroboam.

6. La Bourse et La Vie

12, rue Vivienne, 75002

Daniel Rose's elegant bistro reboot is a reminder that it isn't enough to bring dishes like pot-au-feu, steak-frites, and a wildly delicious chocolate mousse back into the limelight, they have to be exalted to stand out. Rose honors these fundamental dishes by sourcing the best ingredients possible and preparing them with great care and precision.

7. Breizh Café

109, rue Vieille du Temple, 75003

For a taste of Brittany in Paris, this is where you go. This outpost of Breizh kicked off Bertrand Larcher's Parisian family of Breton cafés (the business actually began in Japan nearly thirty years ago) serving simple, organic sweet and savory crêpes (the latter are also known as buckwheat galettes). You'll find classic flavors as well as galette rolls, where the buckwheat dough is folded into mini wraps, with less expected combinations like lobster and Granny Smith apple with a miso-yuzu mayo and a shiitake egg scramble.

8. The Cambridge Public House

8, rue de Poitou, 75003

Modeled after an upscale British alehouse, this North Marais bar was launched by three friends who spent time working in London. It marries the warmth, laid-back service, and snacks of a pub (think: sausage rolls, cheese pasties, and meat pies made with top-shelf French ingredients) with the precision and inventiveness of the world's best craft cocktail bars. Book ahead to guarantee a table (though it is not mandatory) or at least an hour or two on the Chesterfield sofa. Where most bars open at five or six P.M., this one opens at the unusually early hour of three P.M.

9. Candelaria

52, rue de Saintonge, 75003

Candelaria, the taqueria and speakeasy in the North Marais, was at the forefront of both the Mexican food and craft cocktail waves when it first opened in 2011 and remains just as fun and delicious today. If it's your first visit, swing by on Taco Tuesday for a deal on three tacos, and order the Guepe Verte, the house signature cocktail that blends chile-infused tequila with refreshing cucumber and cilantro.

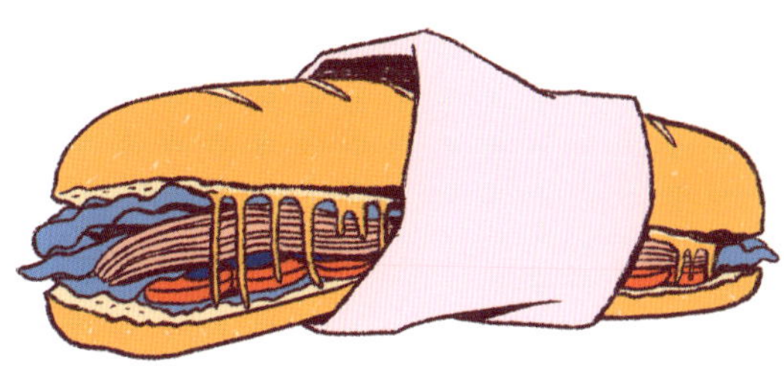

10. Chez Alain Miam Miam

26, rue Charlot, 75003

Alain Roussel is a crêpe-slinging showman nicknamed "le roi du sandwich" (the king of the sandwich) who got his start at a stall in the Marché des Enfants Rouges, where you can still go for his hearty compose-your-own sandwiches and sweet and savory crêpes. At this outpost around the corner, you'll find the same excellent giant sandwiches (shown on page 13) and crêpes, filled with quality ingredients, that earned him a following. At either location, expect a crowd and more than an hour-long wait.

11. Chez l'Ami Louis

32, rue du Vertbois, 75003

The historic, much-debated Chez l'Ami Louis is divisive, with its surly waiters, hefty prices, and compact dining room with only twelve tables. But those who love it (including luxury conglomerate LVMH, which acquired the restaurant in June 2024) will forever wax rhapsodic about the foie gras terrine, potato gâteau, and most notably, the roasted chicken, which is basted in duck and goose fat and presented to the table whole before being plated. Some insist it's the best chicken they've ever had, anywhere. You decide!

12. Chez Denise

5, rue des Prouvaires, 75001

Twenty years ago, Anthony Bourdain called this restaurant "the true and enduring glory of France" on his show *No Reservations*. Today, Chez Denise remains the same relic of Les Halles—the "Belly of Paris"—Bourdain experienced, with unchanged recipes and giant portions of blanquette de veau, venison stew, and haricot de mouton (a medieval mutton and white bean casserole), all served on tables covered in red gingham by career waiters. In case you're looking for a late-night meal, the kitchen doesn't close until eleven P.M.

13. Datil

13, rue des Gravilliers, 75003

Chef Manon Fleury climbed the ranks to become one of the most talented, highly technical young chefs while primarily working in residence at various Paris restaurants. Datil—the name of an ancient variety of plum—is her long-awaited first permanent home with an earthy interior and a largely plant-based and fiercely low-waste tasting menu that gives pride of place to locally sourced ingredients.

14. Les Enfants du Marché

39, rue de Bretagne, 75003

This seafood-centric neo-bistro bar in the heart of the Marché des Enfants Rouges (page 22) is led by a high-energy team of natural-wine enthusiasts, with nonstop service throughout the day. As casual as it is, all that fresh, high-quality fish comes at a price—if you can, splurge on oysters, razor shell clams, sea urchin with white asparagus and a duck-kumquat consommé; a spider crab salad with fava beans, green peas, and wild garlic; and red tuna belly, all prepared by chef Shunta Suzuki. No reservations; get here at the early part of mealtime.

15. Frenchie Bar à Vins

6, rue du Nil, 75002

Gregory Marchand's compact neo-bistro Frenchie put rue du Nil on the map and kicked off his mini empire on the street in 2009. He followed it up with this casual wine bar across the street, a wine shop, and a street food canteen that's since become an Italian trattoria called L'Altro Frenchie. If you want to mix with more locals than foreigners and skip the reservation stress, add the wine bar to your itinerary for wines by the glass from a wide and diverse selection and excellent sharing plates that might include lamb croquettes, seasonal ceviche, veggie tartlets, and the most memorable gougères of any Parisian restaurant.

16. Guefen

9, rue du Vertbois, 75003

This intimate, kosher-friendly restaurant in the North Marais is the first solo project from Israeli chef Ohad Amzallag, whose menu explores the best of French fish and produce, and, most notably, prioritizes fermentation over spice. To sea bream he might add a cream of charred eggplants and cauliflower, with cabbage cooked in espresso and topped with whipped garum (a fermented fish sauce). For dessert, brioche is glazed with miso caramel and served alongside ice cream topped with crumbled shortbread, ginger whipped cream, and candied mint leaf. This unique experience is best enjoyed at the five-seat chef's counter opposite the open kitchen.

17. La Halle aux Grains

2, rue de Viarmes, 3rd floor, 75001

Inside the Pinault Collection at the Tadao Ando–restored Bourse de Commerce building, once a grain and commodities exchange in Les Halles, the legendary chefs Michel and Sébastien Bras draw from the building's past and put ancient grains and legumes in the spotlight at La Halle aux Grains. Overlooking the Saint-Eustache church, this is a full-service, tasting menu situation, not fit for a quick and casual nibble, but a teatime option is available for those in a rush.

18. Juveniles

47, rue de Richelieu, 75001

Since it opened in 1987, this Franco-Scottish bistrot à vins (wine bistro and cave) has been a neighborhood institution, serving unfussy dishes like terrine de campagne, octopus grilled on the plancha, roasted pork rack with a creamy purée and roasted prunes, and an epic cheese selection from both Madame Hisada (located next door) and Neal's Yard Dairy London. Expect an impressive selection of biodynamic and natural wine from around the world.

19. Kunitoraya

1, rue Villédo, 75001

It's thanks to Masafumi Nomoto that Paris fell in love with udon, which he is credited for bringing to the food scene in 1991. Fanatic locals are game to wait in line to get a spot at the communal table (or know to show up right at noon for lunch) to slurp the handmade Japanese wheat noodles in a cold or hot bonito broth. Among the biggest hits are the breaded pork and curry udon, and udon with giant shrimp tempura. Donburi and an array of tapas and saké round out the menu.

20. Liza

14, rue de la Banque, 75002

Few Lebanese restaurants in Paris are as stylish and spacious (and great for families) as Liza, a 2nd arrondissement institution for twenty years with a satellite location in Beirut.

There's a refreshing balance of traditional dishes, such as fattoush and baked kibbeh (shown on page 15), with more contemporary takes, like black-lemon labneh, codfish hummus, sesame-coated tomato jam, and a to-die-for riz au lait (rice pudding) concocted with the help of L'Ami Jean (page 75) chef Stéphane Jégo. For drinks, opt for one of the Lebanese wines or a housemade orange blossom lemonade.

21. Mama Nissa

14, rue Mandar, 75002

Nissa, a nod to the owner's mother, Anissa, whose recipes are served here, is a warm homage to Algerian home cooking. Locals keep coming back for calentica (sometimes called kalantica), a creamy chickpea flour flan sprinkled with cumin; Kabyle couscous with barley, stuffed with herbs and drizzled with a delicious broth and a touch of homemade harissa; and cocas, small turnovers stuffed with vegetables (like the frita, which mixes bell peppers, tomatoes, and onions) or meat. All dishes are available for takeout as well.

22. Mắm from Hanoï

39, rue de Cléry, 75002

With its tender meat, fragrant aromas and spices, and expertly cooked noodles, this spot run by the Hanoï-born couple Tuyet Ngân Bùi and Tuan Anh Tran Luu earned the title of best phở (with a special mention for the phở tái chín, a Northern Vietnamese beef phở) in Paris, first by diners, then by the highly respected guide *Le Fooding*. There are only a handful of phở options on the menu, and they are made fresh in limited quantities, so go early (and add on chà giò, the excellent fried spring rolls). Expect keo lac vung—peanut and sesame candy—with your tea at the end of the meal.

23. Le Mary Celeste

1, rue Commines, 75003

This sea-inspired small plates bar, which also serves small-batch wines and craft cocktails, comes from Quixotic Projects, the group behind Candelaria (page 13). Deviled eggs filled with sesame mayonnaise and topped with fresh ginger, shallots, deep-fried wild rice, and spring onions are the only item that's never left the menu; otherwise, it is ever-changing throughout the seasons, with oysters making their much-awaited return in October.

24. Menkicchi Ramen

41, rue Sainte-Anne, 75001

With only a handful of tables and beer kegs doubling as seats, Menkicchi isn't a place to linger for hours. But it is a standout spot on rue Sainte-Anne, worth a quick visit for tonkotsu ramen. Meat eaters should opt for chef Makoto Saegusa's Spéciale, a generous bowl of handmade noodles in a pork broth, with half a marinated egg, a slice of pork breast, and seaweed leaves, but vegetarians have great options, too.

25. Nhome

41, rue de Montpensier, 75001

As the French-Israeli chef Matan Zaken sees it, guests book their chair, not their table at his tasting-menu-only restaurant facing the Palais Royal gardens. That's because past Nhome's front kitchen and lounge, down a few stairs and into the vaulted stone cellar, you'll find one single asymmetrical, candle-dotted mahogany table that seats eighteen. This won't be your usual communal dining experience—with seats cleverly spaced out and staggered arrival times, you'll hardly notice other diners. Instead, you'll be focused on each of the nine artfully plated dishes prepared using a slew of different textures, temperatures, and cooking techniques, from fermentation to binchotan grilling. Each dish is served and described tableside by a different member of the chef's international kitchen brigade.

26. On the Bab

18, rue Thérèse, 75001

If you see crowds and hear K-pop from the street, you've come to the right place. The restaurateur and entrepreneur Linda Lee brought her London K-food mainstay On the Bab to a minimalist space on rue Thérèse in the Japanese-Korean neighborhood in 2019. You'll find traditional dishes such as Korean barbecue chicken and bibimbap combined with grilled meats, like bulgogi beef and pork with chile, which can be eaten in baos, and fried rice dumplings with kimchi and cheese served with a chile sauce for dipping—all instant hits among locals.

27. Parcelles

13, rue Chapon, 75003

This old-school bistro, a neighborhood institution since 1936 formerly known as Le Taxi Jaune, got a fresh update in 2021 from Bastien Fidelin, Sarah Michielsen, and chef Julien Chevallier, who kept the most compelling original decorative details (stone walls, beautiful floor tiles, and a copper-topped bar) in the now-thirty-two seat bistro. The trio's menu includes dishes like chou farci (stuffed cabbage) in a veal broth, sweetbreads with hazelnut butter set on a mound of luscious mashed potatoes, and a pillowy gnocchi in a butter-sage sauce that's become a house signature. The modern wine list is chock-full of natural and biodynamic bottles (which you can take home with you—just stop into their Épicerie-Cave across the street).

28. La Poule au Pot

9, rue Vauvilliers, 75001

Of celebrated chef Jean-François Piège's reasonably priced establishments, this is the only one that occupies a Parisian bistro fixture with its own legendary heritage. The tableware and kitchen got an update, but the 1930s interiors (think ceramic floor tiles, long banquettes, and globe lights) and a menu devoted to la cuisine bourgeoise (see page 51) were lovingly preserved. Piège revisits a host of classics, from onion soup (shown above) and frog legs en persillade to the namesake dish, bouillon-poached chicken with vegetables, which is served only during the winter. Leave room for the Grand Marnier soufflé. (If the restaurant is full, try booking a table at one of the sister spots in the neighborhood, Clover Grill or À l'Épi d'Or.)

29. Racines

8, Passage des Panoramas, 75002

This "bistrotteria" tucked in the Passage des Panoramas, one of the oldest covered passageways in Paris, is the Sardinian chef Simone Tondo's ode to comforting family recipes. The spot may look like a throwback Parisian bistro (it was once a printing atelier), with aged floor tiles, worn mirrors, and a compact open kitchen, but the dishes lean much more modern: think fresh pasta with beef cheek ragout, vitello tonnato, Milanese-style veal chops, or a seasonal dish of the day, and a truly perfect tiramisu to finish. Expect a predominantly Italian list of natural wines.

30. Restaurant Omar Dhiab

23, rue Hérold, 75001

After perfecting his skills in Parisian fine-dining temples like Lasserre, Ledoyen, and the now-shuttered Loiseau Rive Gauche, Omar Dhiab went solo in 2022 and opened his eponymous modern French restaurant near the place des Victoires. His talent with condiments and sauces is noteworthy—his restaurant earned a Michelin star within six months of opening—as are the subtle nods to his Egyptian heritage like the Karkade (hibiscus drink) that opens the meal and the semolina cake with orange blossom that closes out the experience.

31. Shabour

19, rue Saint-Sauveur, 75002

Shabour is the first fine-dining concept in Paris from the Jerusalem-born chef Assaf Granit. The surprise tasting-menu experience plays out around a granite bar that wraps around the central kitchen, where guests watch as the chefs prepare each dish, not unlike culinary theater but without the gimmick. It's intimate—you'll dine by candlelight—but full of lively energy and multilingual conversation that locals have come to love and expect in a Granit restaurant. For a vegetarian (or vegan, if requested) alternative, head down the street to Tekés, Granit's ode to plant-based cooking, or try Boubalé (page 93), an Israeli take on Ashkenazi food in the Grand Mazarin hotel.

32. Song Heng

3, rue Volta, 75003

At the heart of the city's oldest Chinese neighborhood, Song Heng has been a destination among locals and chefs for Vietnamese bún bò xào (or bo bun, as the locals call lemongrass beef over cold rice noodles) and beef phở. Once you wiggle your way into the compact canteen, all you'll need to do is decide whether you want your dish large or extra-large.

33. Takara

14, rue Molière, 75001

There's no mistaking this traditional Japanese bistro: opened in 1958, Takara is beloved for its sushi, sashimi served on crushed ice with freshly grated wasabi, and nabe—a type of hot pot dish (or as the French call it, Japanese fondue) that you'll be hard-pressed to find anywhere else in the city.

34. Verjus

52, rue de Richelieu, 75001

The American founders of this superb Palais Royal restaurant, accessed via covered passage, showed French diners that their talents could rival any of their French peers when they first opened in 2011. To this day, the nose-to-tail tasting menu emphasizes hyper-seasonal produce (grown in their countryside potager, or kitchen garden) and weaves in diverse flavor profiles and textures. Nearly everything that graces the table is produced in-house, from the sourdough bread and vinegar to the butter and charcuterie. This spot is very accommodating to vegetarians. Don't skip the wine pairing, which is an excellent value.

35. Yam'Tcha

121, rue Saint-Honoré, 75001

Ever since the chef and co-owner Adeline Grattard was featured on her own episode of Netflix's *Chef's Table*, Yam'Tcha has been one of the city's most challenging tables to book. It's worth the hassle for her instinctive cooking that blends French and Chinese ingredients and techniques—everything she loves from those countries. For the full experience, order the signature tea pairing created by Grattard's Hong Kong–born ex-husband, Chi Wah Chan.

1st, 2nd, 3rd, 4th ARRONDISSEMENTS

SHOPPING

As the historic beating heart of the Parisian food world, the neighborhoods encompassing Paris Centre, stretching from the Pont Neuf to the Marais, are understandably rich with specialty grocers, homeware and cookware shops, and destinations for all things sweet—many of which bear a long history. The "lower Marais" is dotted with commercial fashion shops, while the businesses of the "upper Marais" lean edgier, with French-designed wares, concept stores, and craft coffee shops. When you're not à table, reserve time to shop for edible and decorative souvenirs at these fine spots.

1. Astier de Villatte
173, rue Saint-Honoré, 75001
The homewares at Astier de Villatte may look like antiques, but the handmade, pearly ceramics—from dishware and candlesticks to pitchers and teacups—actually borrow from old-world aesthetics and techniques. They're all made by hand in the brand's 13th arrondissement workshops and grace the shelves of this eighteenth-century space, alongside candles, notebooks, and incense.

2. Aux Merveilleux de Fred
24, rue du Pont Louis-Philippe, 75004
An iconic import from Lille with several Parisian locations, Aux Merveilleux de Fred has perfected the merveilleux: a light-as-air mound of layered meringue coated with sweet whipped cream and covered in a variety of toppings, from chocolate flakes to caramelized hazelnuts. Equally divine but lesser known is the cramique, a Belgian brioche bread common to Northern France that you can watch being baked throughout the day.

3. Christophe Louie
12, rue Dupetit-Thouars, 75003
Pastry chef Christophe Louie spent his career in the city's top pastry kitchens and later trained with Mauro Morandin, one of the leading master panettone (Italian Christmas bread) makers in Italy, to expand his repertoire. Since 2018, he's been the go-to for traditional sourdough panettone in Paris through an online shop, but he didn't open his own bakery until 2023. There, he sells hefty sourdough loaves and ciabatta, viennoiseries (breakfast pastries) like the croissant tulipe and glazed madeleines, a heavenly flan, and his signature panettones—classic with fruit and nuts, or with chocolate from the chocolatier Nicolas Berger—prepared fresh daily.

4. E. Dehillerin
18-20, rue Coquillière, 75001
It's no wonder Julia Child adored this more than two-hundred-year-old kitchen supply and cookware store, located on the same corner at the edge of the former Les Halles and with the same facade since 1890. It's a floor-to-ceiling trove of copper cookware, unusual cooking utensils, and baking accessories, and worth a visit even if you don't have a suitcase you can pack full of pots and pans to bring home.

5. Épicerie du Marais
111, rue Vieille du Temple, 75003
Adjoining Breizh Café (page 13), this épicerie-delicatessen is an ideal stop for picking up Breton specialty products, especially if you won't make it to the northwestern coast during your stay. You'll find jams, salted caramel spread, sea salts from Maison Charteau, tinned fish, and a wide selection of farmhouse ciders.

6. Épices Roellinger
51, bis rue Sainte-Anne, 75002
There is no other spice shop worth your time. Run by Mathilde Roellinger, daughter of the beloved Breton chef Olivier Roellinger who started this spice operation more than forty years ago, the shop is a go-to for any serious professional or home cook. Pick up the Roellinger range of top-quality spices in addition to peppers, chiles, cinnamons, chutneys, and a host of other blends.

7. Fou de Pâtisserie
45, rue Montorgueil, 75002
A must for pastry lovers since it opened in 2016, Fou de Pâtisserie was launched by the founders of the country's leading pastry magazine of the same name. Both locations (the other is 36, rue des Martyrs, 75009) feature an exceptional curation of baked goods, pâtisseries, chocolates, and candies from the best pastry chefs and shops in the country, from Pierre Hermé and Nina Métayer to La Maison Angelina and Julien Dechenaud.

8. G. Detou
58, rue Tiquetonne, 75002
Since 1951, this punny shop (pronounced like j'ai de tout—I have everything) has been *the* local reference in professional-grade baking and cooking products at wholesale prices, including baker's chocolate, syrups, candies, olive oil, and condiments. The smaller of two storefronts carries smoked salmon, sardines, cans of foie gras and cassoulet, mustards and other épicerie products that you can easily bring home.

9. Izraël
30, rue François Miron, 75004
Brimming with products from floor to ceiling, this épicerie in the Marais is a treasure trove of spices, condiments, and confit fruit sourced from around the world. Among the 5,000-plus items in stock, be sure to come for the Iranian pistachios, tonka beans (which you can't get in the US), za'atar, candied kumquats, sumac, and more.

10. Kioko
46, rue des Petits Champs, 75002
Since 1972, this specialty grocery store has been a two-story temple to Japanese ingredients and ready-to-eat meals. When you've finished stocking up on dashi, rice vinegar, and miso, you should head to the Marais (20, rue Malher, 75004) for a wide selection of sakés.

11. Legrand Filles et Fils
1, rue de la Banque, 75002
This centuries-old shop, tasting room, and wine bar is accessible from inside the Galerie Vivienne, the most stunning of the city's covered passageways, and delivers the perfect mix of old-world charm and wine expertise if you're looking to linger with a glass and hunt for that elusive bottle from Burgundy.

12. Librairie Gourmande
92-96, rue Montmartre, 75002
Industry professionals, cooking and baking students, history lovers, and bibliophiles alike have flocked to this specialty bookshop since it opened in 1985. The Librairie Gourmande has the city's widest array of multilingual cooking, baking, and oenology books (shown below), alongside historical and scientific reference texts, and food-related literature.

13. Maison Aleph
20, rue de la Verrerie, 75004
Pastry chef Myriam Sabet turned Levantine pastries on their head when she opened this pocket-sized Marais boutique in 2017, offering her take, anchored in French technique, with inventive flavor pairings and made with less sugar. Here, she specializes in shareable seasonal tarts, ice cream, and nids, angel hair nests made of kadaïf (thinly shredded phyllo dough), incorporating clarified butter and filled with flavored creams or candied fruit. Don't leave without taking home a bottle of Damask rosewater syrup.

14. Maison Plisson

93, boulevard Beaumarchais, 75003

Billed as the Parisian answer to Dean & DeLuca (RIP!), Maison Plisson doubles as a specialty grocer and café (or a modestly sized alternative to La Grande Épicerie—page 82). Here, visitors will shop alongside locals for artisanal pantry items and condiments you're unlikely to find anywhere else on the Rive Droite, plus top-shelf dairy and the best produce from small producers across France.

15. Le Marché des Enfants Rouges

39, rue de Bretagne, 75003

The oldest covered market in Paris, this bustling North Marais destination is known for its smattering of specialty stands, from cheese to fish, and food stalls representing cuisines from all over the world. As for the name, it nods to the sixteenth century when Marguerite de Navarre, François I's sister, built a hospice for the sick and orphaned children of Paris, all of whom wore red.

16. Merci

111, boulevard Beaumarchais, 75003

A soaring concept store in the North Marais with two on-site cafés, Merci is as well known for its sharp selection of bohemian ready-to-wear and monthly pop-up installations as it is for design pieces, homewares, and kitchen accessories from indie designers and global brands.

17. Ogata

16, rue Debelleyme, 75003

It may exist within the walls of a seventeenth-century French building in the Marais, previously occupied by a quincaillerie (hardware store), but Ogata is an unmistakable celebration of Japanese craftsmanship, design, and gastronomy. Created by the multi-hyphenate entrepreneur Shinichiro Ogata, the minimalist space spans multiple floors and houses an art gallery, a boutique for homewares and decorative objects, a tea shop and tea salon, a fine-dining restaurant, a whisky bar, and a wagashi counter, which is where you'll find the most budget-friendly items in the store.

18. Plaq

4, rue du Nil, 75002

Just when you think Paris couldn't possibly accommodate more confectionery and chocolate shops, another one comes along with staying power. Plaq is a family-run bean-to-bar shop with top-quality chocolate sourced from Venezuela, Peru, and Belize, then melted and turned into bars (also known as plaques), cookies, cakes, and drinks like chocolate infusions and hot chocolate shots that can be consumed on-site.

19. Sacha Finkelsztajn

27, rue des Rosiers, 75004

Since 1946, the Finkelsztajn family has been the unwavering custodian of this iconic, yellow Jewish deli, renowned for its rugelach, challahs, strudels, and bagels (shown above), as well as cheesecake, cured meats, and smoked and pickled fish. If you go for lunch, don't miss the Yiddish Sandwich, a flavorful blend of red pepper spread, baba ghanoush, and sprats, all nestled within a pletzel—a flatbread sprinkled with onions and poppy seeds.

20. Terroirs d'Avenir

7, rue du Nil, 75002

After getting its start as a supplier to the city's best chefs and restaurants, Terroirs d'Avenir expanded to become the premier green grocer and specialty supplier for locals in 2012. It first left its mark all along on the rue du Nil with a butcher, produce shop, cheesemonger, fishmonger, and bakery, then did the same in the 11th arrondissement.

21. Tomo Pâtisserie
11, rue Chabanais, 75002
On a quiet street in the Little Tokyo neighborhood, this teahouse and pastry shop blends French and Japanese traditions under one roof. On the menu is classic dorayaki (red bean-filled pancake) and a selection of French classics with a Japanese twist: the Paris-Kyoto nods to the Paris-Brest pâtisserie by filling the pancake patties with praline cream made from soba and kinako, while the Dorayaki Baba replaces the rum in a baba au rhum with patties soaked in Nikka whisky. Take them to go with one of the shop's books on Japanese tea culture.

22. Yam'Tcha Boutique
4, rue Sauval, 75001
If you can't get a table at Adeline Grattard's Michelin-starred restaurant (page 18), this is the next best thing. Run by her ex-husband Chi Wah Chan, the boutique does double duty as a tearoom, with a variety of Chinese teas and accessories available to purchase, tastings organized upon request, and a menu of congee, prepared à la minute.

BEYOND RESTAURANTS

Coffee & Tea
Bing Sutt
Café Berry
Café Verlet
Causeries Café & Vin
Dreamin Man Roastery
Fringe
IO Café
Kawa
Laïzé
Motors
Le Peloton
Pontochoux Café
Recto Verso
Télescope
Umami Matcha Café

Bars
Le Barav
Bar Nouveau
Chez Francis
Danico
Golden Promise
Harry's New York Bar
Hoppy Corner
Little Red Door
Serpent à Plume
Sherry Butt

Pâtisserie & Bread
Aki Boulangerie
Brigat'
Bontemps La Pâtisserie
Cédric Grolet Opéra
Cookie Love
Jeffrey Cagnes
La Pâtisserie du Meurice par Cédric Grolet
Pâtisserie Tourbillon
Ritz Paris Le Comptoir
Sain Boulangerie
Stohrer
Takumi Pâtisserie

Ice Cream & Sweets
Baltïs
Berthillon
Boneshaker Doughnuts
Café Isaka
Edwart Chocolatier
La Glacerie Paris
Infiniment Chocolat Pierre Hermé Paris
Jacques Genin
Jade Genin
Jean-Paul Hévin
Pozzetto
Reÿs

A BRIEF HISTORY OF DINING IN PARIS

Paris's reputation as a culinary trailblazer, a European power that set the tone for eating and drinking well, is anything but recent: it didn't begin in the nineteenth century with the pioneering work of chef-author extraordinaire Auguste Escoffier, nor in the eighteenth century with the celebrity chef Marie-Antoine Carême. It was forged over several centuries, beginning in the Middle Ages.

At that time, Paris was part of a thriving viticultural region, including the early sprouts of big houses like Château Haut-Brion in Bordeaux and the rise of Champagne. It may be hard to imagine now, but the city was blanketed in vineyards, and wine production (and moderate drinking—even the bishops and abbots partook!) was heavily promoted during Charlemagne's eighth- and ninth-century reign. As a result, wine became the period's crucial cash crop, a fixture of every royal banquet table and tavern, and an integral part of the local diet. As the city's population swelled throughout the Middle Ages, most of the vineyards all but disappeared.

But wine remained on the table, and the pairing of food and drink was a crucial part of the development of France as a culinary powerhouse. Other staples included eggs and grains, mostly in the form of dark bread soaked in broth, which served as a vessel for vegetables and, on rarer occasions, meat (spit-roasted or stewed beef, mutton, and pork; or peacock, heron, and swan for noble diners). It was flavored with mustard and a plethora of spices, from nutmeg to cinnamon, brought back from far-flung locales. (Aside from the exotic birds, most of the other ingredients are still part of the Parisian table in some form.) The region flourished with vegetables such as cabbage and fava beans between the twelfth and fifteenth centuries (potatoes didn't make an appearance until the sixteenth century), which served as a solid base for nourishing soups and stews.

Variations of this diet existed throughout medieval Europe, but a more distinctive French cuisine emerged by the seventeenth century, says historian Loïc Bienassis. "To a large extent, this benchmark French cuisine can be described as 'Parisian,' because even though the court moved to Versailles in 1682, it was sustained by an essentially Parisian aristocracy."

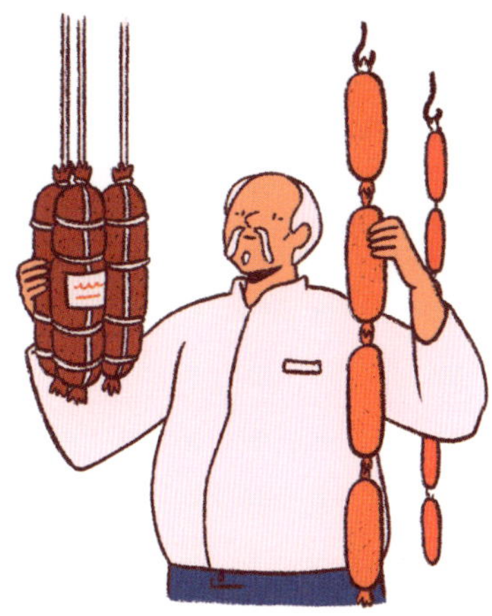

As French cooking was finding its footing, the working-class and local artisans could usually be found dining elbow-to-elbow at the city's many inns and table d'hôtes (the host's table), where a set multicourse meal was served to all guests at the same time, at a fixed price. They relied heavily on the thousands of food and drink shops that had been organized into codified trade associations, by artisans themselves, with strict bylaws—charcutiers were in charge of the sausage and ham trade while bouchers handled all other meat; gingerbread makers and sellers couldn't dabble in other forms of pastry, for example, as the scholar Rebecca Spang describes in her book *The Invention of the Restaurant*. If working-class people were lucky, they had access to meat pâtés, offal, waffles, rissoles, and a host of other ready-to-eat dishes prepared by cook-caterers and itinerant vendors—essentially, the earliest forms of street food. "Chauds pâtés! Chauds gâteaux!" the vendors hawking hot pâtés and hot cakes would shout, emphasizing their temperature to further incite people to buy, particularly during the cold months. The practice lives on today at most open-air produce markets, where merchants compete with one another for a shopper's attention and call out about deals, the juiciest tomatoes, the freshest fish, or the season's last figs.

As a result of the professionalization of food trades, entire streets, some of which no longer exist, became known for their specialties—rotisseries on the Left Bank's rue de la Huchette, sausages on rue de la Saunerie near Châtelet, and bakers along the rue de la Juiverie (named for the robust Jewish community that settled on this street on Île de la Cîté, the island where Notre-Dame now sits).

Meanwhile, the aristocracy and royal court feasted at home. Grand banquets were commonplace and featured a brigade of domestic staff responsible for serving in the French style—each dish brought out on platters simultaneously, displayed at the center of the table, and portioned out for each guest.

Abundance may have been the operative word in the era for an elite slice of the population, but food culture more broadly—the sourcing, selling, discussing, and celebrating—was part of the everyman's daily life. One place in particular became the city's culinary lifeblood: Les Halles.

The history of the central markets at Les Halles extends all the way back to the early twelfth century, when Louis VII created the royal Marché des Champeaux, an open-air market on former marshland along the Seine, outside of the city walls. Les Halles became the main center of trade and commerce for the capital and the surrounding area, and one of the earliest signs of the crucial role that food played in France's national identity. Built upon a foundation of culinary trades (or as the French call them more poetically, les métiers de bouche—professions of the mouth), the markets established a food supply chain and a network of artisans who brought regional cuisines to the big city. The royal court loved to flex the capital's cultural superiority over the rest of the country—something the state is still accused of doing to this day—but the city needed the skills and specialties from the provinces to keep

the market churning. Les Halles was one of the rare places in the city where social classes overlapped to experience the thriving, chaotic, and often seedy bazaar.

By the early nineteenth century, the halls were overflowing and in dire need of an overhaul or a relocation. The architect Victor Baltard was entrusted with the project that led to the area's transformation and constructed twelve iron pavilions with large glass roofs, each housing its own foodstuffs—poultry and game, tripe and offal, seafood, meat, dairy, fruit and vegetables, and even flowers. Shortly after construction, the old corn exchange building from a century prior was repurposed as the Bourse de Commerce (stock exchange) just in time to be unveiled at the Universal Exhibition of 1889.

It was this late nineteenth-century iteration and structure of Les Halles that would become the subject of great fascination for the era's artists, writers, thinkers, and travelers from around the world and anchored Paris to a reputation for all things culinary.

Les Halles, even for those who had never been to Paris, carried an almost mystical air that we can largely credit to Émile Zola's vibrant depictions of the central market and its twelve pavilions in his novel *The Belly of Paris* (1873), considered by many as the first true gastronomic novel. Through detailed, painterly descriptions, Zola not only situated Les Halles as the epicenter of social connections and the most significant source for nourishing the city, but juxtaposed the abundance of goods and the animalistic pleasure they elicit with the jarring suffering and hunger that a large portion of the local population experienced.

The market was fascinating to Zola and his peers for what it conveyed about the political climate and maintaining social peace at the time—this was a period known as the Second Empire, following the French Revolution of 1848, when an authoritarian Napoleon III assumed power and kept a tight grip on the population but also inspired modernity and change. Napoleon wanted Les Halles to be "the people's Louvre," accessible to all. For the first time in hundreds of years, the market was fairly hygienic (but not entirely sans rats), well organized, and well functioning—a symbol of architectural prowess and innovation that nevertheless maintained its village-within-the-big-city spirit. At its peak, Les Halles was the largest food market on the planet.

It remained this heaving food hub for the city until the 1970s, when the traffic congestion around the market and need for repairs became too great and costly to keep it in its original home. It was dismantled and moved outside the city limits to Rungis, where it is currently the largest fresh produce market in the world.

Les Halles wasn't merely the food source for residents, but also for the growing number of restaurants that were taking Paris by storm by the middle of the eighteenth century.

Conventional lore held that the creation of the restaurant was an outcome of the French Revolution, the idea being that the cooks who worked for the aristocracy suddenly found themselves woefully unemployed and took to the streets to "open cafés and sell in public what before you could get only in private," as Adam Gopnik wrote in *The Table Comes First.* And while the revolution may have significantly accelerated the expansion of restaurants, scholars, among them Rebecca Spang, have since disproved this theory, tracing the arrival of the restaurant to the period twenty years prior to the revolution, in the 1750s and 1760s. "Un restaurant" was first a restorative broth or a bouillon (and by extension, a restaurateur was one who repairs or re-establishes) before it was a physical place. An innovation credited to M. Roze de Chantoiseau, the bouillon restaurant, as Spang explains, addressed "a semi-medicinal need in a busy urban setting." The broth was simple and light and served alongside equally light dishes using poultry and eggs, all of which were considered ideal for good health—among the primary obsessions of the elite during the eighteenth century. Naturally, any place serving this healing broth—the era's answer to detox juice—took on the moniker of maison de santé, or health house.

By the 1820s, there were nearly three thousand restaurants in Paris (compared to fewer than two hundred in London and only a handful in New York), and most of the cardinal features we associate with a restaurant today were firmly in place, such as the use of menus, waiters in uniforms, single servings of dishes, intimate dining rooms, table service, and an emphasis on taste over subsistence. These were among the elements that made restaurants uniquely Parisian well into the nineteenth century—there were inns and wine shops beyond French borders but nothing of the sophistication and novelty of Parisian restaurants. "American and English travelers marveled at its restaurants," wrote Spang. "In 1844, John Durbin, president of Dickinson College, wrote of restaurant dining that it was . . . unlike anything he had experienced or witnessed in New York, Philadelphia, or London." It's through this innovation and its nouvelle cuisine that Paris took on the role as Europe's culinary cradle. "The restaurant had become a cultural institution, among the most familiar and distinctive of Parisian landmarks," wrote Spang. It symbolized abundance, a culinary curiosity, and a noticeable shift in culture.

After the French Revolution, restaurants flourished beneath the galleries of the Palais Royal. Among the most prominent and popular was Les Trois Frères Provençaux, run by three brothers from the south of France who brought bouillabaisse to the big city as well as olives stuffed with capers and anchovies, wild duck, and chicken Marengo, said to have been named after one of Napoleon's battlefield victories. The other was Le Grand Véfour, the only nineteenth-century survivor around the Palais Royal gardens, which was known as Colette's canteen. It continues to make appearances in films and television series for its masterfully preserved Directoire-era decor, from the mirrors and woodwork to the crystal chandeliers and plush red banquettes.

The restaurant boom then migrated to the Grands Boulevards, around the rue Montorgueil and the boulevard des Italiens, which had the highest concentration of restaurants in the nineteenth century. Around the turn of the century, their presence extended to the place de la Madeleine and to the Champs-Élysées, where a series of Belle Époque pavilions housed a number

of destination restaurants, many of which, like Lasserre and the Pavillon Ledoyen, are still open today. The other types of establishments familiar to travelers today, such as bistros, bouillons, and brasseries (see pages 63–64), which popped up around train stations like Gare du Nord, Gare Montparnasse, and on the Left Bank on boulevard Saint-Germain, catered to a more working- to middle-class clientele and cast the dining net even wider.

It was during the restaurant's rise that the world's earliest culinary journalists and authors helped to ensure the Parisian food scene's resonance extended far beyond French borders. Were he alive today, Marie-Antoine Carême would have earned the title of food disruptor for his contributions to this pursuit and in doing so, revolutionizing haute cuisine. Thought of as the country's first celebrity chef, Carême cooked for a royal who's-who that included Napoleon, King George IV, and Tsar Alexander I of Russia before going on to establish la grande cuisine and documenting it in 1833's *L'Art de la Cuisine Française au Dix-Neuvième Siècle*. It is Carême who gave the cooking world much of the codified rules of the trade, inventing the soufflé and the éclair, popularizing the classic white chef's toque in the nineteenth century, and developing the four mother sauces—velouté, béchamel, allemande, and espagnole. Nearly a century later, these sauces were adapted to include hollandaise, sauce tomate, and mayonnaise by Georges Auguste Escoffier, another whiz of French gastronomy who gave us *Le Guide Culinaire* (1903) and the kitchen brigade system.

Adding to the canon were Grimod's *Almanach des Gourmands* (1803) and Brillat Savarin's *Physiologie du Goût* (1825), and this written commentary about food as a source of pleasure and national identity was instrumental in exporting French cuisine globally. All of this combined to form what *National Dish* author Anya von Bremzen considers "the first explicitly national discourse about food," and arguably a sense of French culinary exceptionalism that would be both a longstanding source of tremendous pride and, at various points, a tremendous hindrance to change.

Making sense of the evolution of Parisian dining in the nineteenth and twentieth centuries means looking directly at the various waves of migration and immigration that shaped the city. Foreign influence, initially domestic migrants from the provinces, were the locomotives behind the proliferation of brasseries and épiceries (gourmet specialty shops known for spices), and crêperies and pastry shops. They brought the traditions, know-how, and, most importantly, labor that the city so badly needed to function.

Between the 1850s and the late nineteenth century, Paris saw the arrival of the Auvergnats, Bretons, Alsatians, and Corsicans in massive waves, each bringing with them specialties and trades that deeply informed the capital's food landscape. As much as the abiding discourse in France has, as early as the 1789 revolution, emphasized a universalist approach to national identity wherein everyone, regardless of their origins or religious affiliations, is equal in the eyes of the state, the country's long history of immigration has always been fraught with tension. In Paris, that was true as much with the arrival of domestic "others" as with those from abroad.

The Auvergnats fled rural poverty only to find themselves working backbreaking, thankless jobs as water or milk carriers, firewood collectors, and coal vendors in Paris and, like many of the newcomers, treated as outcasts. When France was under the rule of Napoleon III, the Auvergnats set up breweries in the working-class pockets in eastern Paris to sell coal, beer, and wine, and diligently worked to claim an entrepreneurial foothold through the early twentieth century. They struggled to survive through World War I, and by the end of World War II, almost all of the 2,500 cafés, wine bars, and coal merchants present in the city vanished. Ever adaptable, the Auvergnats shifted careers again and took to reviving the bars, tobacconists, restaurants, and hotels that had closed during the war.

The Bretons began arriving in 1865 in the Montparnasse neighborhood with the start of the Paris-Brest train route, and for most, it marked their first time living in an urban area. They engaged in domestic work in the city or physically demanding day labor in the suburb of Saint-Denis and were quickly derided by Parisians for their "country ways," their staunch devotion to Catholicism, and their language (Celtic Breton). In 1898, they were unfairly labeled the pariahs of Paris—an epithet largely attributed to the historian Louis Chevalier. But just like the Auvergnats, the Bretons and Alsatians, including members of the Wepler, Zimmer, Dreher, and Bofinger families, set up their own brasseries and beer operations, all of which still operate today. And those who didn't brew were crêpe-slinging, which is why you'll find just as many crêperies today around the Montparnasse Tower as bakeries or corner cafés. The very first, Ti Jos, has operated continuously since 1937. Joining these regional migrants, which also included the Basques, Normands, Provençaux, and Bourguignons, among others, were those from outside of the country. The work the domestic migrants left behind, as they moved into higher-paying jobs, would eventually be filled by newcomers from abroad. In fact, France became the third-largest host country for European emigrants after the US and Argentina in the late nineteenth century.

It may have been the English, Irish, Scandinavians, and Dutch that took off en masse for the New World in the early 1900s, but hundreds of thousands of Belgians, Germans, Italians (still one of the largest foreign communities in Paris), and Spaniards set their sights on the French capital, a wave of arrivals the entire country needed to shore up industrialization.

The years between the First and Second World Wars saw the next big periods of migration from Portugal, Spain, Poland, Russia, and Armenia—cultures that infused their food traditions and recipes into the evolving Parisian melting pot. It's at this time that cooking magazines and cooking schools started incorporating recipes for curry and dishes à la créole or à l'algérienne drawn from France's colonies. And those colonies, from Morocco and Tunisia to Senegal and Vietnam, among many others, would shape the very meaning of "French food," particularly in the capital.

Diversity further accelerated during Les Trente Glorieuses, the thirty years of tremendous economic growth following the end of World War II, creating an influx of immigration from Spain, Algeria, Portugal, Morocco, Turkey, China, Laos, Vietnam, and Cambodia (part of the former French Indochina, following the Vietnam War), the Levant region, and sub-Saharan Africa by the 1960s and 1970s. Multiple waves of Chinese immigration, which

began in the early twentieth century and continued well into the 1970s, made southern Chinese cooking a defining feature of the food landscape. In the mid-seventies through the 1980s, that shifted to southeastern Chinese, particularly Cantonese, with new arrivals. The community is spread between Arts et Métiers, the historic settling place that some call Little Chinatown (and is still home to a number of long-running and inexpensive canteens like Happy Nouilles, Le Royal China, Le Lac de l'Ouest, and the Sichuan favorite Trois Fois Plus de Piment), Belleville to the north, and the area commonly referred to as Chinatown in the 13th arrondissement. From delis and specialized markets to noodle bars and dim sum restaurants, there is not one neighborhood in Paris today that doesn't reflect the history of Chinese relocation.

None of this was without great friction. As the academic, historian, and former education minister in the Macron administration Pap Ndiaye told the *New York Times* when he was leading the National Museum of the History of Immigration in 2021, the French have long struggled with "picturing their country as a land of immigration," particularly when there was a tacit expectation for immigrants to "forget where they came from, and become more French than the French." Insofar as that applies to the foods of immigrant communities, they largely catered to immigrants themselves throughout much of the twentieth century.

It's been a very long time since Parisian food and dining could be defined exclusively by the dishes, methods, and customs that inspired cooks like Julia Child and M. F. K. Fisher. Today, it is a composite of influences old and new, domestic and foreign. It is the product of both painful and uplifting stories of colonization, immigration, and new beginnings. To know that couscous, burgers, bánh mì, mafe, American southern fried chicken, Kurdish kebabs, and siopao exist in abundance and, most importantly, thrive alongside croque monsieur, croissants, and pot-au-feu, is a testament to the cosmopolitan threads that weave through the city.

Where resistance to change once held the capital back from fully embracing the rich influences of its multiethnic and multifaith population (as did the ill-founded sense that Parisians had perfected all there was to perfect about food and cooking writ large), today it is new ideas and broadened horizons that have enriched local dining in surprising and inspiring ways.

One of the biggest drivers of this evolution was the period of stasis that characterized the dining landscape in the late 1990s and early 2000s. A tradition-minded approach to food, as Adam Gopnik has called it, was increasingly at odds with changing tastes and a rapidly shifting food scene in countries like Spain, Denmark, and Japan. Food critics in the United States published lengthy meditations on the decline of French cuisine and its temples in Paris. Ironically, the weight of that culinary heritage was ultimately holding chefs and restaurateurs back from breaking free from the confines of the past. Parisians may have invented the restaurant, but they weren't pushing beyond the status quo. When Wendell Steavenson wrote in the *Guardian* that "at the turn of the millennium, when Ferran and Albert Adrià at El Bulli in Spain were inventing molecular gastronomy by spherifying melon juice, France's great chef du jour, Joël Robuchon, was perfecting mashed potatoes," she wasn't kidding.

The response to excessively buttoned-up white tablecloth service and a stultified way of cooking came in the form of a movement pioneered by the chef Yves Camdeborde that would later be called la bistronomie or bistronomy (see page 50). Bistronomy offered diners an alternative to classic bistros and ultra fine dining, with menus featuring rigorously seasonal and inventive dishes in casual, pomp-free dining rooms, while also offering chefs a chance to flex their creativity and technical skills without being limited by the old-school rule book. Following in his footsteps were some of the greatest bistronomic (or neo-bistro) chefs in contemporary Parisian dining history—Iñaki Aizpitarte of Le Châteaubriand, Grégory Marchand of Frenchie, Daniel Rose at Spring, Pierre Sang at his namesake restaurants (page 107)—all of whom inspired the next generation of chefs and restaurant owners, like Charles Compagnon of Le Richer and Le 52 (page 101), Tatiana and Katia Levha of Le Servan (page 108), Adrien Ferrand of Eels (page 104),

Manon Fleury of Datil (page 14), and Moko Hirayama and Omar Koreitem of Mokonuts (page 106). Together, they are leaving a lasting mark on the food scene.

At the same time, this market-fresh, seasonal, casual, but high-quality ethos extended to natural wine bars and caves à manger (see pages 53 and 65) that continue to be among the most popular establishments across all twenty arrondissements. The same can be said for street food (see page 58), which includes everything from dumplings and lobster rolls to Levantine pita sandwiches and bibimbap, which has captured an audience of diners interested in unpretentious and creative dishes that are relatively inexpensive. Not only do such foods dominate social media, they have become mainstays of food and music festivals, pop-ups, and even annex ventures from the city's most decorated chefs.

That doesn't mean the classics have lost favor entirely. In fact, more than a decade after bistronomic restaurants spread across the city, there came a considered push to revive old-timey bistros and brasseries with better-quality ingredients, refreshed interiors, and better service. Daniel Rose helped this along with the opening of his intimate bistro La Bourse et

La Vie (page 13), as did restaurant groups like Bouillon (République and Pigalle) and La Nouvelle Garde (Brasserie Dubillot, Brasserie des Prés on page 76, etc.) that have proven consistently good. The valiant return of old favorites had an extra push during the pandemic when diners took comfort in the familiar. That has continued ever since, not only with simple bistros but with experiential dining institutions like La Tour d'Argent (page 47) that are attracting a new generation of curious eaters.

Today, whether it's a twist on the bistro or a natural wine bar-meets-taqueria, every type of restaurant and cuisine has its own legitimate spotlight. Which means dining out in Paris has never been more exciting. Bon appétit!

DINING ETIQUETTE & TIPS

Every culture has its etiquette rules, and respecting them when you travel is a fundamental component to understanding a destination and experiencing the best it has to offer. The French remain quite formal when it comes to greetings and a host of other codes of conduct, so keep these tips in mind as you eat and shop your way through Paris.

Know when Parisians dine
With the exception of a few all-day, nonstop service restaurants (think: Au Pied de Cochon), most establishments stick to set dining hours: noon or 12:30 P.M. to 2:30 P.M. for lunch, and 7:30 P.M. at the earliest for dinner, with a last call for food orders at 10 P.M. Plan on grabbing a snack if you need something to tide you over until dinner time.

Start with bonjour and bonsoir
Of any social transgression, the most egregious to Parisian sensibilities is the lack of a proper greeting. When entering a restaurant, bar, shop, or even the bus, it's crucial to say bonjour, or bonsoir if it's the

evening, before anything else. Have a question but haven't issued a hello? Don't even think about asking it before you open up the exchange with a salutation.

Ask for the bill when ready . . .

"L'addition, s'il vous plaît!" is what you should say when you're ready to wrap up the meal and head back out into the city. With the exception of restaurants that turn tables more strictly when the second seating is about to begin, most consider it impolite to bring the bill before a diner has specifically requested it. Just know you may need to ask more than once for the servers to bring it to you—their urgency is taking the orders and bringing out the food, not rushing you out the door. In most cases, the server or manager will bring a credit card machine to your table for you to pay (cash is also accepted) or will indicate if you should pay at the counter.

. . . and know how to tip

Unlike in the United States, restaurant servers in France earn a salary, paid vacation, and benefit from nationalized healthcare. The 15 percent service compris, which French law stipulates must be included on all restaurant menus, means that 15 percent of the total bill includes a service fee. It does not, despite the common misconception, mean that the tip was already folded in. And tip is *not* required, anywhere (though tipping hotel housekeeping is always a best practice). Nevertheless, if you had a good or excellent experience and wish to leave a little something extra, 5 to 10 percent is more than acceptable. In most cases, you can leave this in cash on the table or request to add it to the total amount when paying by card, but some restaurants and bars have begun using credit card machines that prompt the client to leave a tip when they pay. The tip amounts proposed by the machine start at 10 percent, but you can insert your own preferred amount or bypass this step entirely to complete the transaction.

If you make a reservation, honor it or cancel it

No-shows aren't unique to Paris but represent an ever-growing strain on restaurants. If you book through Zenchef or Google, be sure to check for emails that will prompt you to confirm, adjust, or cancel your reservation in advance. And if there's a last-minute change? Pick up the phone and let the restaurant know.

Chinatown
Latin Quarter
Montparnasse
Val-de-Grâce

5th, 13
ARRONDI

2

th, 14th
SSEMENTS

DINING

1. L'Assiette
2. Baieta
3. Chanceux
4. Chez Mamane
5. Crêperie de Josselin
6. Le Duc
7. La Felicità
8. Hugo & Co
9. Impérial Choisy
10. Juni Armenian Bakery
11. Kitchen Ter(re)
12. Kokoro
13. Mavrommatis
14. MoSuke
15. Nosso
16. Otto
17. Phố Tài
18. Restaurant AT
19. Le Severo
20. Sola
21. Solstice
22. La Tour d'Argent

SHOPPING

1. Les Caves du Panthéon
2. Fromagerie Laurent Dubois
3. Maison Claudel Vin & Whisky
4. La Petite Épicerie de la Tour
5. Shakespeare and Company Café
6. Tang Frères

5th, 13th, 14th ARRONDISSEMENTS

5th, 13th, 14th ARRONDISSEMENTS

DINING

They may border each other, but these three rather large districts on the Left Bank, encompassing the 5th, 13th, and 14th arrondissements, couldn't be more diverse in population and historical significance—from the Asian diasporas that make up the city's largest Chinatown and the students studying at the Sorbonne, to the latter-day intellectuals who once fraternized over coffees and cigarettes at storied cafés.

In the 13th arrondissement around the avenues d'Ivry and de Choisy, where many Chinese and Vietnamese populations settled in the early 1970s, you'll find a mix of specialty regional cuisines from Vietnam, Laos, and Cambodia, though Chinese restaurants are still most predominant today. The Choisy Triangle, formed by the avenue de Choisy, avenue d'Ivry, and the boulevard Masséna, makes up what most travelers know as Paris's Chinatown. It's where some of the most legendary restaurants, traiteurs (delis), and markets opened in the 1970s and 1980s following the largest wave of more than sixty thousand Chinese and ethnic Chinese refugees from Chaozhou and Southeast Asia. They resettled at Les Olympiades, the district's large, modern housing complexes that French buyers shunned, and gradually built up businesses alongside a significant Vietnamese population. Immigrants who didn't find a home there went north, laying down roots throughout Belleville. This is where you'll find a thriving Chinese community with a host of standout restaurants, old and new (as well as its own Lunar New Year parade).

Slightly north and closer to the river, but still in the 13th arrondissement, this area features important transit, cultural, care, and information centers such as the Gare d'Austerlitz, the hub for trains heading to southwestern France; Les Docks, a bright green modern building housing the Cité de la Mode et du Design; and the Bibliothèque Nationale, or "BnF" as it's commonly called, named after former president François Mitterrand.

Head northwest, and before you know it, the high-rises emblazoned with murals by world-renowned street artists disappear and, once again, you're back in the Latin Quarter and the Paris you read about in history books. Looming over it all atop Montagne Sainte-Geneviève—the highest point on the Left Bank—is the Panthéon, which has been the burial place for distinguished citizens such as Victor Hugo and Marie Curie since 1791. The popular rue Mouffetard, a busy market street, slopes southward behind it.

Though the Latin Quarter has long been a destination for students to find cheap eats, more recently options have shifted a bit more upscale. The area gets its name because students were educated in Latin, and while it's still home to the University of Paris (with forty separate colleges, including the Sorbonne), it's now mostly filled with tourists. Blame the Lost Generation artists and writers such as F. Scott Fitzgerald, Ernest Hemingway, Gertrude Stein, and Pablo Picasso, who all made it their stomping grounds—when it was still affordable—before moving out to Montparnasse.

During the height of café society between the wars, the artistic set moved further outward, frequenting spots such as Le Select, La Rotonde, Le Dôme, and La Coupole—the likes of which have been re-created in cities around the world. While the historical glamour of these brasseries remains, they are more famous for their fables than the food served. Since 1973, the garish Tour Montparnasse has anchored the area above the train station, with many Breton eateries nearby as this station services the Brittany region.

1. L'Assiette
181, rue du Château, 75014
When you imagine hearty, generous French fare, your mind should take you to some version of L'Assiette. David Rathgeber's traditional bistro, with a semi-open kitchen and spectacular painted ceiling, pays homage to the classics of yesteryear, like escargots, braised beef stew, calf's head (tête de veau), and the city's best cassoulet.

2. Baieta
5, rue de Pontoise, 75005
At Michelin-starred Baieta in the Latin Quarter, Julia Sedefdjian—the youngest chef in France to have her restaurant awarded a Michelin star—has made a name for herself with her bright and creative Niçoise cooking. Prepare for dishes like crispy egg yolk with raw and cooked haddock, a sea bream tartare with lime served with a side of lobster in a coconut milk broth, and her signature bouillabaieta, a take on bouillabaisse (the traditional fish stew), made with monkfish, scorpion fish, and squid and served in a velvety rouille (shown below).

3. Chanceux
63, rue Galande, 75005
This is the second spot from Thomas Lehoux, one of the city's OG specialty coffee stars, and cook Farah Laacher. The focus here is coffee, freshly pressed juices, cakes, and mammoth made-to-order sandwiches (get the mushroom melt or schnitzel). For longer hours and access to rare wines, visit their first location in the 11th arrondissement at 57, rue Saint-Maur.

4. Chez Mamane
27, rue des Cinq Diamants, 75013
A few steps from the Butte-aux-Cailles, the 13th arrondissement's picturesque hilltop neighborhood full of narrow cobblestone streets, Algerian couscous and street art come together in surprising ways at this nearly thirty-year-old bistro. Regulars dig into merguez, lamb, or "royal" couscous (page 54), often with a view of stencil work from Miss Tic or a fresco by students from a nearby design school.

5. Crêperie de Josselin
67, rue du Montparnasse, 75014
It's hard not to love this Breton-run crêpe icon near Montparnasse, as much for its rustic wood-paneled and lacy decor as for its purist buckwheat galettes and wheat-flour crêpes served on antique tableware.

6. Le Duc
243, boulevard Raspail, 75014
When the seafood institution Le Duc opened in the late 1960s, it broke with convention by ditching the heavy sauces and overwrought plating to focus on simplicity and the quality of its wild catches. (It also went rogue on the decor, decked out to this day like a vintage yacht.) Raw and lightly cooked fish abound, but sauces make an appearance for the signature main: cutlets of John Dory fish coated in vodka-butter sauce.

7. La Felicità
5, Parvis Alan Turing, 75013
This massive food hall run by the Big Mamma Group (a well-funded collection of sharply designed and affordable trattorias that revolutionized Italian cuisine in Paris) is housed in Station F, France's tech incubator and the world's

largest start-up campus, in the 13th arrondissement. Eight different dining stands await, each done up in colorful neon, including a pizzeria, a trattoria, a gelateria, an Italian cocktail bar, a caffè, a biergarten, and a burger joint. Come in the evening for a decidedly more animated vibe as live music and DJ sets usher diners to the dance floor in the wee hours.

8. Hugo & Co

48, rue Monge, 75005

One of the best contemporary bistro values in Paris can be found at the French-Cambodian chef Tomy Gousset's second restaurant. Located across from the Lutetia Arena (ruins of a Roman amphitheater in the Latin Quarter), Hugo & Co is the more affordable little sister to Tomy & Co, with a seasonal menu that's great for pescatarians and a few meaty standouts like steamed bao with oxtail, pickled vegetables, peanuts, and coriander.

9. Impérial Choisy

32, avenue de Choisy, 75013

This family-run Cantonese restaurant has been a 13th arrondissement institution since it opened its doors in 1981. Line up alongside regulars for greatest hits like jellyfish salad, ginger chicken, pan-fried prawns, and five-spice Peking duck.

Skip the wine and drink Tsingtao beer, as locals do.

10. Juni Armenian Bakery

79, rue Daguerre, 75014

After years working in French bakeries, Grégory Guerguerian opened Juni, the city's first Armenian bakery-deli hybrid, to reconnect with his origins and celebrate Armenian culinary traditions. Lahmacun (flatbreads also known as "junis") come flat or rolled and are available with meat, veggies, or cheese, along with salads, cheese boreks (phyllo dough turnovers, shown above), marinated hot dishes, and gata (a sweet, flaky pastry) for dessert.

11. Kitchen Ter(re)

26, boulevard Saint-Germain, 75005

William Ledeuil, best known for Ze Kitchen Galerie (page 79), takes his passion for cooking with Southeast Asian flavors and applies them to a menu built around ancient-grain pastas and broths. Seafood has a strong presence on the menu, but the vegetarian dishes, like Khorasan wheat elbow pasta with shiitake mushrooms, spinach, kimchi, and parsley green curry dressed with a mushroom vinaigrette, are knockouts.

12. Kokoro

36, rue des Boulangers, 75005

After cutting their teeth with Alain Passard at L'Arpège (page 75), Sakura Mori and Frédéric Charrier set out on their own with a discreet mid-range restaurant in this quiet pocket of the Latin Quarter. The pared-back simplicity of the space belies the complexity of each plate's flavor and technique, which extends to the organic sourdough bread made in-house. The à la carte menu includes a handful of standouts, including the foie gras crème brûlée with a peanut praliné, a venison stew in a chestnut jus, and poached Normandy scallops flavored with shoyu and herb-infused butter.

13. Mavrommatis

42, rue Daubenton, 75005

The Mavrommatis brothers aren't only known for their range of excellent Greek yogurts, fetas, and condiments, carried in every Parisian grocer, but for the delis and restaurants they've run for the last forty years. With one Michelin star, this is the crown jewel, highlighting chef Andréas Mavrommatis's beautifully presented Hellenistic cooking shored up with traditional French techniques.

14. MoSuke

11, rue Raymond Losserand, 75014

Mory Sacko, the city's biggest breakout star, may be gradually building his dining empire, but the restaurant that started it all is MoSuke, which earned a Michelin star within two months of opening in 2020. Here, Sacko draws the inspiration for his singular cooking style from his French-West African origins as well as a deep reverence for Japanese produce and culinary techniques. Imaginative flavor pairings are executed with great skill in one of the most beautiful, contemporary Left Bank dining rooms.

15. Nosso

22, promenade Claude Lévi-Strauss, 75013

This second restaurant from the Brazilian chef Alessandra Montagne (shown above), set in an ultra-modern building directly across from the

Bibliothèque François Mitterrand, has the same zero-waste culinary ethos as Tempero, Montagne's spot next door. That means nose-to-tail cooking and local sourcing (up to 90 percent from the region) drive dishes like her signature carrot focaccia lined with thin strips of bottarga and sorrel leaves in a carrot purée or pork confit on a bed of sweet potato purée and farofa, a toasted manioc flour side commonly found in Brazil. Another bonus: she serves nearly a dozen wines by the glass if you're not up for ordering a bottle.

16. Otto

5, rue Mouffetard, 75005

A no-reservation organic wine bar-meets-izakaya with seats surrounding a central open kitchen and barbecue, Otto is the award-winning chef Eric Trochon's (see Solstice, page 47) valiant attempt at zhuzhing up the dining options in a notoriously touristy stretch of the Latin Quarter overflowing with forgettable to-go joints and all-day cafés. If dining with a group, ask about booking the private-party room that seats up to sixteen guests.

17. Phố Tài

13, rue Philibert Lucot, 75013

If there's any phố worth traversing the city for, it's the perfectly layered, spicy, and creamy phở satay, with tender beef, garlic, and peanuts, served at Phố Tài. Since the 1980s, chef Te Ve Pin—who moved from Vietnam in 1968—has cultivated a following that includes locals, the diasporic community, and even "godfather of French cuisine" Alain Ducasse.

18. Restaurant AT

4, bis rue du Cardinal Lemoine, 75005

Counted among the city's most avant-garde chefs, the Japan-born Atsushi Tanaka fuses the diversity of his cooking experiences—having worked everywhere from Pierre Gagnaire in Paris to Geranium in Copenhagen and Oaxen Krog in Stockholm—for a culinary style without clear definition. You will sense, however, his influences span molecular, Nordic minimalism, and classic French, in a dining room done up in Danish-inspired furnishings and

dishware from his favorite Scandinavian ceramicists. A surprising touch for coffee service: he only offers the pour-over method.

19. Le Severo

8, rue des Plantes, 75014

Butcher-restaurateur William Bernet's intimate bistro hasn't changed much in the more than thirty years since he first opened Le Severo in a residential pocket of the 14th arrondissement. The menu is reliably short and fully meat-focused, featuring boudin noir (blood sausage) and charcuterie to start, followed by steak tartare, dry-aged faux filet (sirloin), prime rib, or veal chops served with thick fries or green beans, and only two options for dessert: crème caramel or chocolate mousse. There will be no regrets, whatever you order.

20. Sola

12, rue de l'Hôtel Colbert, 75005

Sola was one of the earliest restaurants in Paris to masterfully bridge the richness of French terroir and the precision of Japanese cooking techniques with its poetic omakase menu (shown above). Today, chef Kosuke Nabeta offers eight tightly choreographed courses at lunch (Friday and Saturday only) in the vaulted cellar, where guests take their shoes off and sit on a cushion on the ground for a Japanese-style meal. The ten-course dinner (available with wine or saké pairings) takes place in the more formal dining room. Both are brilliant but long experiences, so plan accordingly.

21. Solstice

45, rue Claude Bernard, 75005

One of the most respected chefs in Paris, Eric Trochon's one-Michelin star restaurant demonstrates the merit of the Meilleur Ouvrier de France title he earned in 2011—one of France's highest culinary honors. Run with his sommelier wife, Mi Jin Ryu, Solstice is elegant without being intimidating. The couple offers two menus, including an omakase option, that highlight Trochon's wide-reaching influences. Expect dishes anchored in French technique but inflected with Japanese and Korean touches.

22. La Tour d'Argent

15, quai de la Tournelle, 75005

This 442-year-old restaurant overlooking the Seine and the Notre Dame Cathedral is as iconic for its panoramic views from the sixth-floor dining room as it is for its food and record-breaking cellar of wines, 300,000 bottles deep. The menu was revamped several years ago but still includes the pressed duck or "duckling Frédéric Delair," which is carved directly at the table. Each duck is numbered, and the dish is presented with an embossed souvenir card, a tradition started by the maître d'hôtel from the nineteenth century who made his namesake dish a signature. For three generations, the Terrail family has preserved this Left Bank wonder, and it continues to keep up with the times—in 2023, André Terrail opened an all-day café and bar on the ground floor and made forty-five seats on the seasonal rooftop available for an al fresco cocktail or glass of bubbly.

5th, 13th, 14th ARRONDISSEMENTS SHOPPING

The diversity of these arrondissements is reflected in their sheer variety of specialty stores, from pâtisseries and wine cellars to bookstores and cheese shops. Some may look like they could be run-of-the-mill neighborhood establishments, but walk through the entrance and you'll discover what makes them special—and why they're often destinations in and of themselves.

1. Les Caves du Panthéon
174, rue Saint-Jacques, 75005
A block from the Panthéon, this beloved neighborhood shop might look classic but is, in fact, a destination for an exceptional and unconventional (read: natural, biodynamic, funky, or rare) selection of French and European wines. Come to buy a bottle or stay to try them at cellar price.

2. Fromagerie Laurent Dubois
47, ter boulevard Saint-Germain, 75005
This is cheese ground zero, the flagship location for the award-winning fromager and affineur Laurent Dubois, who also holds the title of Meilleur Ouvrier de France (MOF). His best-in-industry cred is palpable in the selection of premium and rare cheeses, many aged on-site, and dairy products. Taste test a few aged Comtés before you buy, and don't miss his creative cheeses, where flavors like wine must, hay, and chile pepper are added through preservation techniques.

3. Maison Claudel Vin & Whisky

62, rue Monge, 75005

The focus of this Latin Quarter shop is right in the name. Take a further look and you'll see that it more than delivers on the promise of wine and whisky with more than 300 wines from across France and 300 whiskies sourced from international distilleries and independent producers—all of which can be served and sipped on-site, in addition to a robust selection offered by the glass.

4. La Petite Épicerie de la Tour

13, quai de la Tournelle, 75005

Not everyone has the desire or budget to dine at La Tour d'Argent (page 47) but they can still bring home an edible memento from the restaurant's specialty shop. Here, you'll find jams, spices, and condiments, foie gras and terrine, tea and biscuits, and wines ranging from the eminently affordable to the old and rare (shown opposite).

5. Shakespeare and Company Café

35, rue de la Bûcherie, 75005

The city's most iconic English-language bookstore has the perfect place to kick back with a book—right next door. The Shakespeare and Company Café, run in collaboration with Marc Grossman's Bob's Bake Shop (see page 84), serves golden chai, specialty coffee, and veggie and vegan snacks baked fresh from Bob's and Ten Belles. Another bonus: unobstructed views of Notre-Dame.

6. Tang Frères

48, avenue d'Ivry, 75013

You may not plan to do much cooking while you're in Paris, but it's worth visiting the country's pioneering pan-Asian grocer, with its sprawling selection of products and snacks from China and Thailand. At this historic location, opened in 1976 by Chinese-Laotian brothers, you'll also find Tang Gourmet, a traiteur full of ready-to-eat dishes and sandwiches.

BEYOND RESTAURANTS

Coffee & Tea

Cayo Café
The Coffee
Crible
Hexagone
Loutsa
Strada

Cocktail & Wine Bars

Bar des Maillets d'Argent
Bonvivant
Café de la Nouvelle Mairie
L'Entrepôt
Les Papilles
Solera

Bread, Pâtisserie & Sweets

Le Boulanger de la Tour
Boulangerie Archibald
Pâtisserie Carl Marletti
Choco au Carré
La Maison d'Isabelle
Pâtisserie de Choisy
La Petite Alsacienne

PARIS ESSENTIALS

What do we consider essential in Paris? Concepts, culinary movements, and themes, as you'll read below, that we think every traveler to Paris should know in order to truly understand the fabric of the city.

BISTRONOMY

A neologism of bistro and gastronomy, the bistronomy genre reflects a shift initiated in the 1990s by the chef Yves Camdeborde, who wanted to offer an alternative to the stiffness, high prices, and white-tableclothed standards of haute cuisine. In stripping back the experience and focusing on top-quality and traceable ingredients, including many forgotten (and more affordable) vegetables like Jerusalem artichokes, rutabaga, and kohlrabi; simpler plates; and more casual service in comfortable, pomp-free interiors, Camdeborde and his disciples were able to make gastronomic dining accessible. Iñaki Aizpitarte, Grégory Marchand, Daniel Rose, Pierre Sang, and an entire generation of chefs with training in the country's award-winning kitchens, as well as a desire to break out on their own, followed in Camdeborde's footsteps and went on to launch a full-fledged food movement. Neo-bistros, as they're called, are also characterized by open kitchens, creative and rigorously seasonal menus with broad influences that change weekly if not daily, a largely low-intervention wine list, and staff kitted out in jeans, sneakers, and linen aprons. While they initially came up in the 11th arrondissement, at **Le Châteaubriand** (page 103), **Septime** (page 108), **Pierre Sang** (page 107), **Au Passage**, **Clown Bar**, and **Le Servan** (page 108) as well as other parts of eastern Paris, where rent was cheaper and chefs with modest budgets could keep costs tight, they have since proliferated throughout the city.

Au Passage
1, bis Passage Saint-Sébastien, 75011

Clown Bar
114, rue Amelot, 75011

BOULANGERIE & PÂTISSERIE

If bakeries dot nearly every corner of Paris, it's because bread—buying it and pairing it with nearly every meal—is fundamental to daily life. But not all are created equal: some specialize in bread as a primary trade but also sell baked goods (such as viennoiseries, page 66) and fine pastry while others are wholly devoted to bread. But to be called a boulangerie, the bakery must, by law, make all of its bread on the premises from raw, never frozen, ingredients. Similarly, for a shop to be called a pâtisserie, where it produces more involved and technical pastries, it must employ a maître pâtissier, or master pastry chef. For more on Paris's baking culture and rich pastry heritage, see page 138.

LA CUISINE BOURGEOISE

Pot-au-feu (a slowly simmered meat and veggie stew), boeuf bourguignon (a hearty stew of beef braised in red wine), chou farci (cabbage stuffed with ground meat)—these are all dishes that have become staples of bistro dining and fixtures of cookbooks like *Mastering the Art of French Cooking*. They are examples of la cuisine bourgeoise, a type of cooking that may sound fancy but really describes family-style home cooking—rich and hearty slow-cooked dishes anchored in local ingredients, with recipes that date back to the nineteenth century. When modernist cooking became de rigueur in the 1970s and 1980s, the elite world of Michelin-caliber fine dining cast off these essential dishes as ugly, indigestible, old-fashioned, and out of touch with the way Parisians wanted to be eating.

While these unpretentious dishes might not be built around aesthetics and were indeed, at one point, ill-suited for the modern-day restaurantgoer who wanted to be surprised and expected lighter and more creative fare, they didn't stay away for long. After the bistronomy boom filled a gap between cheap eats and fine dining, with its pared-back dining rooms and seasonal and inventive dishes at accessible prices, the scene was ripe for a bistro revival.

La cuisine bourgeoise returned to the forefront in 2015, roughly a decade after Yves Camdeborde took the chance on nostalgia with **Le Comptoir du Relais** in the 6th arrondissement (after spearheading the bistronomy movement with his peer Bruno Doucet long before that). Its resurgence is largely thanks to the French-trained American chef Daniel Rose, known first in Paris for his modern spot called Spring (now closed) and later **La Bourse et La Vie** (page 13), his intimate bistro full of velvety banquettes. As modern as his cooking was at Spring, he never abandoned the past. As he put it at the time, "French cooking didn't get exported all over the world because it was bad. It happened because it was delicious and the people making it were onto something," said Rose in an interview in 2016. His vision was always anchored in Escoffier's mother sauces and classic recipes. What he so beautifully accomplished at La Bourse et La Vie and, by extension, at his New York restaurant Le Coucou, was to update it but keep it nourishing. Substantive dishes like artichoke salad with foie gras, céleri-remoulade, steak-frites, and chicken fricassée in a red wine sauce have all graced the menu and been embraced by diners. As a result, plenty of other classic bistros rooted in la cuisine bourgeoise traditions have proliferated across the city: **Le Bon Georges**, **Le Bistrot Paul Bert** (page 101), **Les Arlots** (page 101), **Bistrot des Tournelles** (page 12), and **L'Assiette** (page 44). At first glance, the award-winning neo-bistro **Septime** (page 108) smacks heavily of Nordic inspirations, but with further inspection, you'll find old-world features of "bourgeois" cuisine woven into Bertrand Grébaut's creative carte blanche menu, like eggs en meurette (the Burgundian dish of poached eggs in red wine sauce), and riffs on the blanquette de veau (a veal stew with carrots and leeks in a creamy white sauce). All of these establishments are a reminder that even in the birthplace of haute cuisine, there is a lasting place for elevated home-style cooking.

Le Comptoir du Relais
9, carrefour de l'Odéon, 75006

Le Bon Georges
45, rue Saint-Georges, 75009

WINE BARS

The only Parisian pastime that might rival dining out is hopping between wine bars. Generally compact, with only a smattering of tables or bar seats, a modest menu of snacks and small plates, and stocked to the brim with bottles, the wine bar can provide a pre-meal apéro (see page 63), a tapas-like dinner, or a post-meal tipple. Some are offshoots started by well-known chefs and restaurateurs—think: **Frenchie Bar à Vins** (page 14), **Septime La Cave**, or **Freddy's** (page 77)—but plenty are stand-alone destinations run by wine experts with strong points of view and thoughtful (and occasionally experimental) selections. For more about drinking in Paris, see page 115.

Septime La Cave
3, rue Basfroi, 75011

NORTH AFRICAN CUISINE

Much of the food, culture, and lifestyle in Paris is the reflection of its deep cross-pollination with Algeria, Tunisia, and Morocco, former French colonies and protectorates known jointly as the Maghreb. North Africans began arriving in Paris in the 1920s, settling around the 18th and 19th arrondissements, and that migration accelerated in the post-war years, once France established a labor policy to recruit foreign workers in a widespread effort to rebuild the French economy. Members of the diaspora have set up businesses all across the city, running couscous restaurants, pâtisseries, and specialty grocers, but the neighborhoods of Belleville, Ménilmontant, and Barbès-Rochechouart continue to be the biggest hubs for all manner of North African culture.

The most traditional and long-running establishments have helped uphold the status of couscous as one of the most prized dishes in the entire country, so if that's what you're after, head to **Le Tagine** (page 108), a Moroccan restaurant known for its natural wine list and selection of couscous and tagine dishes. There's also **L'Homme Bleu**, a Berber restaurant in the 11th arrondissement that's been family-run for more than forty years. Its signature is the couscous royal, an entirely French invention named for its mixture of meats—typically lamb, chicken, and merguez sausage. There's also the street-art inflected **Chez Mamane** (page 44) in the Butte-aux-Cailles neighborhood, and the institution restaurant **Mansouria** (page 106), whose owner Fatéma Hal wrote *the* book on couscous and can tell you everything there is to know about the dish. But for lesser-known recipes that showcase Maghrebi cuisine in all its richness, you'll want to direct your attention to a few others. **Majouja**, a coral-hued canteen in the 9th arrondissement, has become the go-to for amekfoul, a Kabyle couscous with broad beans and peas, topped with a hard-boiled egg and olive oil, as well as rechta, a super-fine Algerian pasta in a turnip cinnamon broth, crowned with a tender chicken leg.

Cantine Yemma, Mustapha Khalis's Moroccan restaurant, was among the earliest to bring Moroccan street food to the forefront in Paris, beginning with event catering, then a food truck, followed by two casual restaurants. At Cantine, Khalis puts forward a selection of kémias (mezze) and turns msemen, Maghrebi flatbread, into meat or veggie kazdal sandwiches, in addition to serving couscous and tagine classics. Chef and TV personality Abdel Alaoui took a page from Yemma and opened his own Moroccan canteen, **Choukran,** in the 9th arrondissement but gave it a slicker, design-forward interior and family-style menu. Recent openings such as these signal a long overdue departure from the traditionalist focus that has long defined North African cuisine in the city.

L'Homme Bleu
55, rue Jean-Pierre Timbaud, 75011

Majouja
43, rue Laffitte, 75009

Cantine Yemma
119, rue du Chemin Vert, 75011

Choukran
29, rue Saint-Georges, 75009

LEVANTINE CUISINE

If there's anything that has taken over as the cuisine de rigueur in Paris in the last eight to ten years, it's the flavors of the Mediterranean and the Levant. The popularity of Levantine cuisine, with all of its influences, skyrocketed after Yotam Ottolenghi and Sami Tamimi's global bestseller *Jerusalem* was translated into French in 2013. Since then, the book (plus Ottolenghi's subsequent adaptations) has sold more than 500,000 copies in France and left a lasting mark not only on what people were cooking at home but what ingredients they could access, as supermarkets and specialty grocers began adding a greater diversity of spices, pantry items, and prepackaged hummus and tahini to their shelves.

In short order, a clutch of restaurants anchored in Levantine tradition popped up across the city: a first outpost of Eyal Shani's **Miznon**, the pita sandwich favorite from Tel Aviv located around the corner from **Tavline**, an Israeli canteen. Chef Assaf Granit's co-owned JLM Group swooped in thereafter with a mix of high and low restaurants like Balagan (now called **Kapara**), **Shabour** (page 18), **Tekés**, **Shana**, and **Boubalé** (page 93); chef Liran Tal runs a semi-gastronomic experience with a vast array of Mediterranean and Levantine wines at **Alluma**; while the **Le Daily Syrien** and **Urfa Dürüm** (page 109), have made Syrian and Kurdish sandwiches part of the daily diet.

Liza (page 15) puts the spotlight on classic Lebanese dishes, and chef Alan Geaam, who went from being an undocumented worker after arriving from Lebanon to building a wildly successful restaurant group, has generated a loyal following at his street food establishments and namesake one-Michelin star restaurant (page 132), built on the Lebanese culinary repertoire. Meanwhile, chef Rita Higgins demonstrates the breadth of flavors and influences that make

up contemporary Lebanese cooking at **Kubri** (page 106), with nods to her previous experiences cooking in Japan. Perhaps no sweeter update to Levantine pastry exists than Myriam Sabet's **Maison Aleph** (page 21), where shareable tarts, ice cream, flavor-filled nids (kadaïf angel hair nests), and reinterpreted baklava combine with the fundamentals of French pâtisserie.

Miznon
Multiple locations

Tavline
25, rue du Roi de Sicile, 75004

Kapara
9, rue d'Alger, 75001

Tekés
4, bis rue Saint-Sauveur, 75002

Shana
14, rue Saint-Sauveur, 75002

Alluma
151, rue Saint-Maur, 75011

Le Daily Syrien
Multiple locations

SOUTHEAST ASIAN CUISINE

Among the most prevalent cuisines in Paris, the abundance of Southeast Asian food is a direct reflection of France's colonialization of Vietnam, Laos, and Cambodia, three of the countries that were part of what was formerly referred to as French Indochina. Learn more about the influence of Southeast Asian food on page 67.

SUB-SAHARAN AFRICAN AND CARIBBEAN CUISINE

There may have been migratory waves of Malians, Senegalese, and other sub-Saharan Africans as far back as the end of World War II and through the 1970s—another example of colonial ties—but the cuisines of these cultures didn't get the focus they deserved until far more recently. Read more about the past and present of sub-Saharan African and Caribbean food on page 156.

JAPANESE CUISINE

Ever since diplomatic ties were signed between France and Japan in 1858, there has been a veritable love affair between the two nations. The late nineteenth century marked an incredible period of discovery of Japan among foreigners, which, after years of isolation, was no longer as closed off to the outside world. French luminaries, including composer Claude Debussy, poet Charles Baudelaire, and artists Claude Monet and Edgar Degas, all found themselves influenced by the works of art, from ceramics to woodblock prints, that made their way to France. "Japonisme" came to describe this far-reaching influence of Japanese culture on everything from Western literature and art to fashion and gastronomy.

In foodways, French kitchens were impacted as well. A report for Eater published in 2017 attributes many of the tenets of the French nouvelle cuisine movement in the late 1960s to key techniques and aesthetics of Japanese food that the movement's pioneers—Paul Bocuse, Jean and Pierre Troisgros among them—learned on a trip to meet Shizuo Tsuji, a Francophile, culinary ambassador, and founder of one of Japan's most well-known cooking schools. If multicourse small dishes became commonplace in French fine-dining temples, it's largely due to the influence of that visit and the chefs' introduction to kaiseki, Japan's traditional multicourse dinners. In Paris today, this influence is still seen in street food, noodle canteens, and mini-marts as well as Japanese-run neo-bistros, upscale sushi bars, and inventive pastry shops. "Japan is a country of specialists because they're all shokunin [loosely defined as a craftsman] while every French person was born holding their umbilical cord and a 150-year-old family recipe for daube [a classic French stew]," jokes food writer Jonathan Nunn of the newsletter Vittles. In other words, underlying the Franco-Japanese connection is a mutual obsession with mastery and tradition, pursued with monomaniacal focus.

It's no wonder so many Japanese chefs operate in Paris, which continues to offer one of the best culinary educations in the world. For decades, Japanese chefs have come to master the foundations of French cooking and perfect their skills in the country's top kitchen brigades. What's more recent is that they choose to stay on and build their careers in the capital. Some uphold the ceremonial, fine-dining tradition when they open their own restaurants, such as Ryuji Teshima of **Pages** (page 132) or Kei Kobayashi of **Kei** (he is the first Japanese chef in France to be awarded three Michelin stars—see Splurges, page 136), while others like Sota Atsumi of **Maison** (page 106) and Sho Miyashita of **Haikara** (page 105) riff on the informal bistro or the izakaya, blending the best of French and Japanese cuisines and ingredients in creative ways.

LA STREET FOOD

Long before NYC had its hot dog carts and food trucks, Paris had its own version of street food. As far back as the Middle Ages, paupers cooked innards in water basins, and prepared the period's equivalent to fast food: warm meals like wafers and rissoles (meat and spice patties coated in breadcrumbs and fried), served in baskets lined with fabric. They were peddled in the streets or at Les Halles market. Today, apart from the falafel sandwiches of the rue des Rosiers, which are often consumed while walking or perched on the edge of a curb, what is considered street food is not literally prepared nor consumed in the street or while walking. What la street food equates to today is a mix between fast-casual and trendy fast food, and a whole lot of takes on fried chicken: karaage at **Nakatsu**, Korean BBQ at **SAaM**, buttermilk-marinated at **Dogma**, and American soul-food style at **Gumbo Yaya**. Most importantly, it's still, more often than not, eaten while sitting down.

One of the most ubiquitous forms of street food in Paris is le kebab, also known as le grec, le döner, le dürüm, or le shawarma. The etymology of the sandwich, with meat or vegetables stuffed into a pita, comes from Turkish döner. They were initially more common in the banlieue and working-class neighborhoods on the fringes of the city, where you could get one with a drink and fries for less than 5 euros in the 1990s. The working-class favorite turned cultural icon is now found in more than five hundred spots in the city in different iterations, some served up in hole-in-the-walls using frozen ingredients, some using only high-quality meat and vegetables in a more thoughtfully designed space. But only in France will you sometimes see the kebab called "un grec," a reference to the Greek gyro, served in a pita with tzatziki, which arrived with the first Greek immigrants to the Latin Quarter during the interwar years.

The adaptations and variants you'll find across town include le döner kebab (the most classic, with lamb and/or chicken stuffed into a pita with tomatoes, onions, lettuce, and often fries, and topped with white sauce), le dürüm (a Kurdish rolled sandwich made with unleavened flatbread and filled with finely chopped grilled skewer meat and vegetables), the Berliner kebab (carved meat, crudités, grilled vegetables, and feta in a pita), and shawarma (spit-roasted lamb or chicken in a pita, with vegetables and sometimes tahini or hummus). **Özlem** (page 107), **Sürpriz**, **Mehmet** (page 151), **Gemüse**, and **Broche** are some of the best places to try these varieties.

Nakatsu
25, rue Ramey, 75018

SAaM
59, bis rue de Lancry, 75010

Dogma
10, rue des Petites Écuries, 75010

Gumbo Yaya
3, rue Charles Robin, 75010

Sürpriz
Multiple locations

Gemüse
61, rue Ramey, 75018

Broche
49, Passage des Panoramas, 75002

VEGETARIAN AND VEGAN

Paris may not be a temple to plant-based eating just yet, but it has made tremendous strides in the last ten years, building on the work of early risk-takers who offered vegetarian dishes before it was "popular." It's possible to trace the start of veggie consciousness to Michelin-caliber chefs such as Michel Bras in the Aubrac, who offered the first all-vegetable menu option in 1978. That's also the year that Paris got its first fully vegetarian restaurant with **Le Grenier de Notre-Dame** in the 5th arrondissement, which is still open today. Aside from naturally vegan dishes such as falafel, veggie couscous, dumplings, and phở (*if* they do plant-based broths), it wasn't until the 2000s that a slew of veggie canteens began popping up. Unfortunately, most were basic and bland at best, without a true culinary vision or sense of highlighting, à la Ottolenghi, all the many ways vegetables can be the star of the show. That started to change with the 2007 opening of **Sol Semilla**, a vegan canteen along the Canal Saint-Martin with hearty dishes rooted in Amazonian superfoods, like cacao and maca, that its founder had started importing years before.

The English-French couple Rose and Jean-Charles Carrarini highlighted mostly vegetarian dishes and breakfast culture when they opened the first **Rose Bakery** (page 86) in 2002. (A string of tearooms and a grocery followed.) Hearty porridge, eggs, and buttery scones for breakfast sat alongside square-shaped vegetable quiches, colorful mixed salads, and big bowls of roasted vegetables and grains at lunch that Parisians were more than happy to queue up for. Still, it would be years before the diversity and versatility of plant-based dishes would reach a wider audience.

The arrival of the naturopath and caterer Angèle Ferreux-Maeght in 2015 helped this along. Having spent time in the slow-food capital of San Francisco, she returned to Paris to launch **La Guinguette d'Angèle**, a vegan to-go window in the 1st arrondissement, at just the right time—Parisians were increasingly focused on health as well as food sourcing and traceability and welcomed her with curious (if not fully open) arms. **Jah Jah** (page 105) really shook things up in 2016 with Afro-vegan recipes that were completely novel to most diners: puréed black-eyed peas topped with jerk-roasted red kuri squash, okra, and sauce chien (a Creole hot sauce); chickpea stew with peanut sauce, jollof rice, and plantains; veggie mafe (peanut stew) or Jamaican curry; and even deconstructed vegan hot dogs—all tributes to recipes drawn from the owners' Afro-Caribbean origins. That the canteen doubles as an unbearably hip streetwear destination (it has become a hub for sneaker culture through the owners Coralie Jouhier and Daquisiline Gomis's limited edition designs in collaboration with the brand Salomon) has only helped to enhance the appeal of vegan cooking.

The vegan-as-healthy-and-clean philosophy has found its own following through **Wild & the Moon**, a local chain of cafés known for its cold-pressed juices and shots, vegan salads, and dairy- and meat-free takes on classics like grilled cheese, burgers, and the bánh mì; and **Maisie Café**, a popular vegan and gluten-free canteen in the fashion-forward center of town.

Meanwhile, the restaurateur Alice Tuyet has been working tirelessly to normalize the idea that eating masterfully prepared vegetables in a festive and joyful environment doesn't require a vegan label. She began modestly with **Plan D**, a seasonal vegan sandwich counter near the Canal Saint-Martin before opening the two-story plant-based **Faubourg Daimant** that looks and feels as warm and inviting as any other contemporary bistro in Paris.

Then there are the restaurants and cafés that don't necessarily brand themselves too heavily as vegetarian or vegan but have become popular for their menus that are suitable for all diners, like **IMA**, an Ottolenghi-inspired vegetarian bar along the Canal Saint-Martin, and **Kitchen**, a popular breakfast restaurant in the Marais. That also extends to non-French restaurants such as **Kubri** (page 106) and **Le Tagine** (page 108), whose menus are

full of vegetarian-friendly options. The vegan movement has also found a place in bars and sweet shops: There's **Abricot**, a plant-based craft cocktail bar with vegan snacks; **Boneshaker**, Amanda Bankert's vegan doughnut shop (frequented by Ina Garten); and **VG Pâtisserie** in the 11th arrondissement—the first to veganize fine pastry, from the Paris-Brest to the flan. Even the French food legend Alain Ducasse produces several vegan-friendly chocolate bars at each of his chocolate shops (page 111), including one made with a coconut milk base. Strict vegans should seek out **Land & Monkeys**, the country's first all-vegan bakery brand, from Rodolphe and Yoshimi Landemaine, founders of the wildly successful group of Landemaine neighborhood bakeries. As longtime vegans, the couple knew there was a business opportunity, as long as it wasn't too preachy. Key to their success has been creating shops that approximate, both visually and in terms of offerings, modern French bakeries and eschew the word "vegan," which still makes much of the dining public bristle. Instead, you'll see "végétal" (plant-based) displayed discreetly on windows.

As for finding vegetarian options at most restaurants and bistros, it's getting easier (the same cannot be said for vegan fare just yet, unfortunately). Guests can usually find one or two vegetarian options on a menu but should call ahead to tasting menu restaurants to request a full vegetarian option.

Le Grenier de Notre-Dame
18, rue de la Bûcherie, 75005

Sol Semilla
23, rue des Vinaigriers, 75010

La Guinguette d'Angèle
34, rue Coquillière, 75001

Wild & the Moon
Multiple locations

Maisie Café
32, rue du Mont Thabor, 75001

Plan D
22, rue des Vinaigriers, 75010

Faubourg Daimant
20, rue du Faubourg Poissonnière, 75010

IMA
39, Quai de Valmy, 75010

Kitchen
74, rue des Gravilliers, 75003

Abricot
189, rue Saint-Maur, 75010

Boneshaker
86, rue d'Aboukir, 75002

VG Pâtisserie
123, boulevard Voltaire, 75011

Land & Monkeys
Multiple locations

PARISIAN FOOD GLOSSARY

The terms below pop up frequently throughout the book and are crucial for every traveler, diner, and Paris lover's dining vocabulary.

Apéro (or Apéritif): This is both the name of a drink and a cocktail hour. The apéritif (or apéro, as locals say) is a touchstone of French culture. It begins in the late afternoon as a means of opening up the belly for dinner, pairing easy-to-drink and/or low ABV drinks with light snacks, and can stretch well into the evening, sometimes even replacing a proper meal.

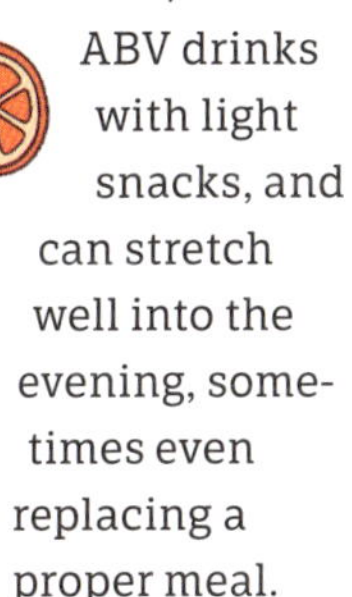

La Baguette Tradition: Baguettes may be quintessentially French, but they are not all created equal. The "baguette tradition," or "tradi," emerged in the 1980s as an alternative to the increasingly low-quality, mass-produced, and bland white baguette. These artisanal versions are made from a sourdough starter, formed by hand (hence the occasional irregularity in the loaves), and baked on-site. Most importantly, the bread can contain only four ingredients—flour, leavening, water, and salt—to be considered a "pain de tradition française," as stipulated by the 1993 Bread Decree. La tradition is the true choice when you're off to buy a baguette for your Parisian Seine-side picnics, apéro cheese boards, or road-trip sandwiches.

Bistro: If the brasserie is bustling and full of life, the bistro is smaller and more intimate, with service restricted to mealtimes. It also offers a tighter menu, built around heartier, slow-cooked dishes like pot-au-feu, cassoulet, sweetbreads, and all manner of regional stew (think: boeuf bourguignon) that found its way to Paris during the migratory waves from the French provinces during the nineteenth century. Decoratively speaking, this is where the checkerboard tablecloths, zinc countertops, and chalkboard menus of popular imagination may make an appearance.

Bo Bun: You'll see this southern Vietnamese dish, which Eater has referred to as Paris's unofficial official dish, listed on restaurant menus all across the city (and not only in Vietnamese spots but

Cambodian, Laotian, Chinese, and even some French cafés). The dish, otherwise known as bún bò xào or bún thịt nướng in Vietnam, features cold rice vermicelli noodles topped with stir-fried lemongrass beef (popular among French diners) or grilled pork (the more common version in Vietnam) and typically served with fresh lettuce, cucumbers, mint, cilantro, bean sprouts, pickled carrots, crushed peanuts, and a nước chấm sauce. You'll typically find it topped with fried spring rolls (pork or veggie-based), referred to as nems instead of the Vietnamese chả giò.

Bouillon: As a type of restaurant, the bouillon predated the explosion of the Parisian bistro in the nineteenth century and was known largely for its spacious dining room; hearty, simple, and very inexpensive dishes; and quick service for working-class diners. Depending on the historical source, some say it was the entrepreneur Baptiste-Adolphe Duval who opened the first one; others say it was the butcher Pierre-Louis Duval who did so as a means to use up and sell all the bas morceaux (the least desirable cuts from the front of the cow), prepared in several formats, including in their broth—a bouillon. The bouillon faded in popularity in the early 1900s, until 2017 with the opening of Bouillon Pigalle, and later, Bouillon République (page 13).

Brasserie: The brasserie is typically a spacious restaurant with soaring ceilings and ornate Art Nouveau-era decor that serves a wide range of dishes, from deviled eggs to lobster, continuously from early morning to late at night. These spaces first emerged with the arrival of Alsatians who sought refuge in the capital after fleeing the Franco-Prussian War. Naturally, they brought their most prized local traditions along with them: brasserie means "brewery," so these establishments were not only places to eat and socialize but where beer was made on the premises.

Café: At its start, the café was an all-day public space where coffee was served alongside the daily newspaper and heated debate. It wasn't until after the French Revolution, when a decree made it legal to consume and serve wine and spirits

along with coffee under the same roof, that the offerings expanded. Most importantly, the café represented a third place that appealed to intellectuals, artists, and writers. Today, it remains a democratic, open-to-all space for conversation and inexpensive drinks. As for the food, it's all over the place, with croissants and soft-boiled eggs in the morning and then omelets, croque monsieurs, basic salads, and burgers the rest of the day.

Cave à Manger: A hybrid wine and small-plates bar with a particular liquor license that requires guests to order food if they intend to drink. The wine selections are typically very reasonably priced, and dishes may vary in their level of sophistication. In a place like La Buvette (page 116), you can expect plump olives, chicken liver terrine, and white broad beans in olive oil, while at Le Verre Volé (page 109), one of the earliest examples of the cave à manger (opened in 2000), you can make a meal out of the outing.

Épicerie: Essentially a gourmet grocer, the épicerie can be traced back to the Middle Ages, when it was defined as a small shop specializing in spices sourced from around the world ("épices" means spices). Over time, other foodstuffs were added to the mix, and owners began packaging their own products and slapping their names on them. By the end of the nineteenth century, there was a network of namesake, family-owned shops across the country. Traditional épiceries declined throughout the twentieth century as they were folded into big hypermarchés like Carrefour; today, they're making a comeback thanks to young upstarts.

Le Pâté en Croûte (or Pâté-Croûte): It may be centuries old, but this forcemeat pie, made with a mix of finely chopped and seasoned meat, wrapped in puff pastry dough, and baked until golden, has never been more popular with Parisians.

One of the first documented iterations was published in *Le Viandier de Taillevent* in the fourteenth century, which is one of the oldest compilations of medieval recipes. Then, the dish was a practical means of using up leftover meat and preserving it in a pastry casing that wasn't meant to be eaten. By the Renaissance, buttery crusts became edible and encased a host of additional fillings, from pistachios to truffles. Chefs working for the royal court adored making them for the element of surprise during service: Slicing into these dough-covered mounds revealed elegant layers and patterns.

Saint-Honoré: The creation of the Saint-Honoré pastry in 1847 is credited to chef Auguste Julien of Maison Chiboust (then located on rue Saint-Honoré), and was meant to honor the patron saint of bakers. Initially presented in the form of a brioche filled with cream, it evolved into the cake we know today, composed of a puff pastry base, chiboust cream (pastry cream and Italian meringue), chantilly, cream-filled choux, and a caramel shell. According to Pierre Hermé, "the Saint-Honoré is the very symbol of pastry-making expertise, bringing together the great classics of the trade: puff pastry, choux pastry, two types of cream, cooked sugar, and poaching." You'll find a mix of the classic version at bakeries across the city, including Stohrer, and more original twists, either in flavor or presentation, at Carl Marletti, Cédric Grolet, Pâtisserie Rayonnance (page 155), and Pierre Hermé (page 81).

Viennoiserie: This term refers to breakfast pastries made in the Viennese style that fill the gap between fine pastry (pâtisserie) and bread. Take the croissant: Its ancestor is the Austrian kipferl, a brioche-like bread in the shape of a crescent moon with a varnished crust. It is thought to have arrived in Paris with the establishment of German and Viennese bakeries in the 1830s and was later adapted to the buttery, flaky iteration we know today in the late nineteenth century. Pains au chocolat, chaussons aux pommes (apple turnovers), and brioches are all considered viennoiserie and are not only consumed in the morning but typically as a late afternoon snack—even among adults.

SPOTLIGHT: SOUTHEAST ASIAN CUISINE

The prevalence of Vietnamese, Laotian, and Cambodian restaurants in Paris is a direct result of French colonialism in these countries, each a part of what was formerly known as French Indochina. The first waves of Vietnamese immigration pre-dated the fall of Saigon, making France home to the oldest Vietnamese diasporic community. Some 50,000 Vietnamese were recruited as workers and soldiers during the First and Second World Wars and decided to stay in the country. The more significant migratory wave came in the mid-1970s as refugees from Vietnam, Laos, and Cambodia fled war and communist regimes. While Southeast Asian populations have historically called the 13th arrondissement home, their reach today extends across the city, with many restaurants run by second-generation folks in their thirties and forties. **Tan Dinh** (page 79), opened in 1968, is the oldest Vietnamese restaurant in Paris. It's been run by two brothers, who took over from their mother in the late 1970s, and is known for bánh cuốn-esque smoked goose ravioli made with glass noodles that pair beautifully with rare French wines.

Julien Pham, the French-Vietnamese restaurant consultant, roving restaurateur, and founder of the creative food agency Phamily First, believes the younger generation is revolutionizing Southeast

Asian food for the capital—a shift that is long overdue.

"Restaurants today are much closer to their true identities [and what you'd find in Asia] than they were during our parents' wave of immigration," says Pham. "There was a whole generation of restaurateurs, particularly Chinese and Southeast Asian, who completely adapted their cooking to the Parisian palate. As a result, they've generated new recipes that aren't reflective of traditional Asian cuisine but which have become hybrids—bo bun is one such example (see page 63). They did this because survival was their priority. They had been forced to leave their homelands. Naturally, they were committed to fitting in and not rocking the boat when they settled in Paris.

"As a result, the city ended up with restaurants that made little sense from a cultural point of view. In one establishment, a menu could have Chinese, Thai, and Vietnamese dishes as a way to accommodate the Parisian dining audience who long lumped all Asian cultures and cuisines together. Unfortunately, that created a standard for most Asian restaurants in Paris and the loss of each country's cultural identity, along with a litany of clichés. They all look the same, they all taste the same, they all cost the same.

"The shift now is that many of the long-running restaurants have been taken over by the younger generation, who are finally ready to assert their culture and regionality. **Lao Siam** (page 173) on rue de Belleville is a good example: brothers Nicolas, Frédéric, and Alexandre Souksavanh took over from their parents, who set up this Laotian-Thai institution in 1985, and brought the restaurant up to date by simplifying the menu and concentrating on core dishes like banana blossom salad and suea rong hai, or 'crying tiger.' The menu used to be a bible plopped on the table; now it's a two-pager with a more limited geographical scope. They've kept a few outlier dishes, like the bo bun, but have made it far more culturally consistent.

"Next door, their sister restaurant, **Ama Siam** (page 171), is an ode to their mother's cooking; what they ate at home. I didn't only eat Vietnamese at home growing up—my mother sometimes made Chinese or Cambodian dishes. So the brothers allow themselves this 'transgression,' so to speak, through the story of their mother's home cooking. The sisters who own **Double Dragon** (and Le Servan, page 108) completely refocused on their French-Filipino origins after being open for several years and running as a kind of 'New

Asian' restaurant, weaving in the plurality of their personal influences. In all these examples, they're championing their heritage with a greater sense of urgency than ever before."

Some of Julien's other favorites include **Ngoc Xuyen Saigon**, on rue Caillaux; **May Hong**, located in the Olympiades shopping complex; **Phở Cổ** for Northern Vietnamese cuisine; and **Viahe Caphe**, a coffee shop in the 11th arrondissement inspired by Vietnamese street cafés.

Double Dragon
52, rue Saint-Maur, 75011

Ngoc Xuyen Saigon
4, rue Caillaux, 75013

May Hong
Galerie Olympiades, Centre Commercial Oslo, 44, avenue d'Ivry, 75013

Phở Cổ
142, boulevard Masséna, 75013

Viahe Caphe
16, rue Daval, 75011

A note about Indian cuisine

Paris may be spoiled for choice when it comes to non-French restaurants, but that hasn't included Indian food, which has long been reduced to what's available in the Little India neighborhood behind the Gare du Nord, spanning the 10th and 18th arrondissements. One such hub off the rue du Faubourg Saint-Denis is the covered Passage Brady, built in 1828 and designated a historical monument. The passage is lined with restaurants, spice shops, and beauty salons with a local following. (Despite the name, most of the establishments in Little India are actually owned or run by residents from Pakistan, Bangladesh, or Sri Lanka.) It's only in the last few years that new openings have sprouted in other parts of the city, from modern takes on traditional recipes at **Delhi Bazaar** (page 103) in the 11th arrondissement to Indian regional cuisines at **Sharmaji** (page 78) in the 15th arrondissement, helping to expand the cuisine's audience.

Faubourg Saint-Germain
Pasteur
Saint-Germain-des-Prés

6th, 7t

ARRONDI

3

n, 15th

SSEMENTS

SHOPPING

1. Alléno & Rivoire
2. Barthélémy
3. Le Café Pierre Hermé
4. Chapon Chocolaterie
5. Chartreuse
6. Debauve & Gallais
7. Fromagerie Quatrehomme
8. Des Gâteaux et du Pain
9. La Grande Épicerie
10. Madame Cacao
11. Maison Vérot
12. Marin Montagut
13. Patrick Roger
14. Poilâne

6th, 7th, 15th ARRONDISSEMENTS

DINING

1. L'Ami Jean
2. L'Arpège
3. Augustin Marchand d'Vins
4. Les Avant-Comptoirs
5. Le Bar des Prés
6. Brasserie des Prés
7. Brasserie Lipp
8. Café des Ministères
9. Chakaiseki Akiyoshi
10. Colorova
11. Cravan
12. Freddy's
13. Huitrerie Régis
14. Joséphine Chez Dumonet
15. Le Jules Verne
16. Localino
17. Milagro
18. Oktobre
19. Pilgrim
20. Quinsou
21. Sauvage
22. Semilla
23. Sharmaji
24. La Table d'Aki
25. Tan Dinh
26. La Vera Pizza Napoletana
27. Ze Kitchen Galerie

6th, 7th, 15th ARRONDISSEMENTS DINING

This swath of Paris—especially the 6th arrondissement, with its rare booksellers and gothic churches—is among the oldest and most historic. It's also where you'll find many of the city's well-known and revered points of interest, including Madame Eiffel herself.

The uneven cobblestone streets of Saint-Germain-des-Prés, with a church off the main boulevard that dates back to 1050, is perhaps most familiar to travelers thanks to nearby iconic relics like the Café des Deux Magots, Café de Flore, and Brasserie Lipp, all social haunts among intellectuals and philosophers during and after World War II. All of these spots are still operating (and finding their way into blockbuster films and series like *Emily in Paris*) and have been joined by a growing crop of neo-bistros, specialty shops, and wine bars. The dining scene may not be able to compete with the disruptive bistronomic stronghold in eastern Paris, but what Saint-Germain lacks in of-the-moment restaurants, it makes up for in quality and charm.

Continuing west along the river, you'll pass the former train station-turned-museum, the Musée d'Orsay, and enter the Faubourg—or "outer"—Saint-Germain neighborhood. Fans of impressionism have been visiting this landmark and peeking between the hands of its famed river-facing clock since 1986.

Further west, as you near Les Invalides (originally founded by Louis XIV as a home for veterans in 1671 but now an armament museum that houses Napoleon's tomb) and the Eiffel Tower, the restaurants become either more classic or more expensive—this area is home to L'Ami Jean, Alain Passard's L'Arpège, and the grande dame at the Eiffel Tower, Le Jules Verne.

1. L'Ami Jean
27, rue Malar, 75007
Originally a Basque pub in the 1930s, this 7th arrondissement standout is chef Stéphane Jégo's ode to bistronomic cooking with hearty, American-style portions and a spirited vibe. At wooden communal tables, you'll tuck into technical but not overly precious dishes that have made L'Ami Jean something of a cult Parisian favorite, like ris de veau, pork belly and lentils, gâteau basque, and a gargantuan rice pudding—the chef's signature.

2. L'Arpège
84, rue de Varenne, 75007
Chef's Table star Alain Passard of the triple-Michelin-starred restaurant L'Arpège is best known for having abandoned meat and taken a risk—long before anyone else dared to—on an all-vegetarian menu option (shown above). Divisive many years later for a host of reasons, including repetitive dishes, price, and service, the restaurant generates a lot of love-it-or-hate-it sentiments. But if budget and interest allow, go forth and try out what may just be the most decadent vegetarian tasting menu in the world.

3. Augustin Marchand d'Vins
26, rue des Grands Augustins, 75006
See the red neon sign in the window? You've come to the right place—not a high-energy hangout but a terrific wine bar with soft lighting, exposed wood beams, exceptional bottles of natural wine lining the shelves along an exposed stone wall, and only a handful of marble tables for lingering. Come for a tasting, pick up a bottle, or nibble on quality charcuterie, vegetables straight from the farmer's market, and a couple of warm dishes. Better yet, come for all three.

4. Les Avant-Comptoirs
3, carrefour de l'Odéon, 75006
These are the icons of the neighborhood, a duo of bustling, standing-room-only tapas bars originally launched in 2010 by bistronomy pioneer Yves Camdeborde. The menu of hot and cold snacks is showcased with hanging pictorials; eating and drinking elbow-to-elbow with strangers until the bars close at eleven P.M. is part of the charm. There's another location nearby at the Marché Saint-Germain.

5. Le Bar des Prés
25, rue du Dragon, 75006
The celebrity chef Cyril Lignac is behind a number of stellar restaurants and bakeries, but his grip on Paris is particularly strong on this street, home to four of his latest bars and restaurants. Bar des Prés is both a cocktail and sushi-sashimi bar, with a sizeable menu of shareable plates like seared chūtoro (bluefin tuna), with jalapeño vinaigrette and crunchy radishes, and yuzu-marinated sea bass with miso and rocoto pepper. Known for his pastry, Lignac makes a dessert course you can't overlook that might include ice cream mochi or matcha chiffon cake.

6. Brasserie des Prés

6, cour du Commerce Saint-André, 75006

You'd be forgiven for thinking this cobblestone passageway, lined with cafés and institutions like Le Procope, is a tourist trap. It certainly was at one point, but the Nouvelle Garde restaurant group transformed one massive restaurant space there into its latest modern, all-day brasserie, with fun decor, simple but well-executed classic dishes from the cuisine bourgeoise repertoire (beef tartare, trout en croûte, braised chicken in vin jaune, plus plenty of terrine and pâté en croûte), and jovial service. After you eat, head upstairs to the second floor to Grouvie, the craft cocktail spot where you can sip and dance until late.

7. Brasserie Lipp

151, boulevard Saint-Germain, 75006

With the exception of the merch for sale, little about this late-nineteenth-century brasserie on the boulevard Saint-Germain has changed. The decor is frozen in time, with wrought iron racks for one's top hat or coat and signs indicating proper attire (wearing shorts is verboten!). The servers are still gruff, and the sauerkraut and sausage and potatoes frequently ordered by Hemingway remain menu headliners. Regulars know that the only acceptable seats are in the front portion of the restaurant or on the covered terrace: the far back room is nicknamed Purgatory, and the upper floor is Hell, so choose accordingly.

8. Café des Ministères

83, rue de l'Université, 75007

To understand the lasting legacy of Paris bistros, visit an exemplary one like Café des Ministères, the dining highlight in this administrative pocket of the city (the National Assembly is a block away). Husband and wife duo Jean and Roxane Sévègnes run a small dining room but serve big, marvelously executed favorites like Normandy scallops and chou farci. Be on the lookout for the vol-au-vent, a bowl-shaped pastry shell filled with lobster or a mix of veal sweetbreads, free-range chicken, and spinach and truffle jus.

9. Chakaiseki Akiyoshi

59, rue Letellier, 75015

On a nondescript street behind a nondescript wooden façade sits France's first restaurant devoted to the traditional Japanese tea ceremony (shown above). Where most fine dining tables run by Japanese chefs in Paris flex a mastery of French culinary technique, Yuichiro and Misuzu Akiyoshi double down on kaiseki, the ancestral progression of small dishes that inspired the capital's own model of haute cuisine in the 1960s. Only a handful of guests are served per seating; reservations are crucial.

10. Colorova

47, rue de l'Abbé Grégoire, 75006

This long-running neo-bistro by the innovativ e pastry chef Guillaume Gil serves a vibrant, seasonal lunch menu with two, three, or five-course options during the week. Saturday shifts to a sharing plates format, with an array of vegetable, fish, and meat dishes, before going full brunch on Sunday—complete with a savory main (chicken-kimchi soup, Japanese fried chicken, or homemade meatballs), a sweet side (get the brioche French toast), and a choice between six different elegant pâtisseries.

11. Cravan

165, boulevard Saint-Germain, 75006

Saint-Germain's most unique watering hole is unquestionably this five-story outpost of Franck Audoux's small-but-mighty 16th arrondissement bar Cravan. Here, take your pick between three different bars, each with its own distinct decorative scheme, where you can cozy up for a craft cocktail and selection of elevated bar snacks, like a veggie pissaladière (a fish-free twist on the Niçoise flatbread), onsen tamago (soft-cooked egg in soy broth), lobster rolls, and plenty of dips. A handful of cocktails are bottled and available to take home. And don't miss the Rizzoli bookshop on the third floor.

12. Freddy's

54, rue de Seine, 75006

A Parisian wine bar from the owners of Semilla (page 78) that's open daily, including Sunday and Monday, is a rarity worth noting. Even better when it's a neighborhood mainstay like Freddy's, known for its wide selection of wines by the glass, seasonal tapas menu, and international crowd. Walk-ins only.

13. Huitrerie Régis

3, rue de Montfaucon, 75006

Parisians love oysters, and they especially love fresh-shucked oysters sourced directly from Brittany producers, served at this eighteen-seat raw bar in Saint-Germain. You can start with smoked scallops or caviar and then dive right into the main attraction with platters ranging from Fines de Claire (a less fleshy and low-iodine variety) to plump Belon oysters (also known as flat oysters), served alongside perfectly paired wines. No reservations.

14. Joséphine Chez Dumonet

117, rue du Cherche-Midi, 75006

This century-old bistro is an institution for a reason. Beyond the decorative classicism—lace curtains, bentwood chairs and banquettes, and frosted glass partitions—it maintains a following for its greatest hits menu, also available as half-portions: stuffed morels, roasted langoustines with lemon butter, beef bourguignon, duck confit, and for dessert, a not-to-be-missed Grand Marnier soufflé.

15. Le Jules Verne

6, avenue Gustave Eiffel, 2nd floor, 75007

Dining at the Eiffel Tower is, in fact, all it's cracked up to be thanks to chef Frédéric Anton, who took over the kitchens in 2019 in a space spectacularly reimagined by the architect Aline Asmar d'Amman. Expect five- or seven-course set menus that highlight the excellence of French seafood. Reservations are a must.

16. Localino

10, rue de l'Odéon, 75006

When you've had enough French fare, come to this wine lover's osteria full of flavorful antipasti, fresh pasta, and a superb selection of Italian wines, which are hand-selected by owner Michele Andreoli and are rarely found elsewhere in Paris. The dining room is quiet at the back and more lively toward the front, particularly around the red marble central kitchen island—the best seat in the house.

17. Milagro

85, avenue Bosquet, 75007

New Americana meets Parisian neo-bistro at chef Justin Kent's Milagro, a block from the École Militaire. The New Mexico–born and French-trained chef infuses a refreshing cross-section of flavors from his experiences for dishes like wild fish ceviche with leche de tigre; rack of lamb served with a cauliflower emulsion and sprinkled with Hatch chile; and a silky pumpkin crémeux with ice cream, prunes, and streusel. Even better: It's all served in a bright, beautiful dining room.

18. Oktobre

25, rue des Grands Augustins, 75006

What was once William Ledeuil's Kitchen Galerie Bis—a more affordable sister restaurant to his fine-dining spot Ze Kitchen Galerie (page 79)—was passed down to one of his longtime chefs and mentees, Martin Maumet, who turned it into the well-priced neo-bistro Oktobre. In a warm space with earthy colors, meant to reflect that balmy moment between end of summer and the start of autumn, Maumet celebrates seasonality and his passion for condiments (line-caught whiting fish might be served with artichoke jus, celery root, and cabbage, with pop from yuzu kosho—a Japanese seasoning made from a fermented paste of chile peppers, yuzu, and salt). Overall, it's a beautiful ode to French products and East Asian influences.

19. Pilgrim

8, rue Nicolas Charlet, 75015

The 15th arrondissement is unlikely to ever be considered a dining destination, but if there's one place worth the journey west of the Eiffel Tower, it's this one. Japanese chef Yurika Kitano delivers a memorable gastronomic experience with incredible precision and top-notch produce, fish, dishware, and service.

20. Quinsou

33, rue de l'Abbé Grégoire, 75006

The terroir-obsessed chef-butcher Antonin Bonnet puts the best of France on display at his intimate restaurant a few blocks from Le Bon Marché. Every dish of his prix-fixe menu is bright, thoughtfully executed, and delicately presented, but a few that have gone above and beyond are the Mesquer hay-aged pigeon served with smoked beets and drizzled with a Madeira sauce at the table; marinated mackerel and a pared-back garnish of hazelnut and chile in a wasabi cream sauce; and a superb compilation of multicolored honey-roasted carrots in apple cider vinegar.

21. Sauvage

55, rue du Cherche-Midi, 75006

Despite its informal first impressions—an earthy color palette, rough-hewn blonde wood furnishings, and a palpable laid-back cool—there is serious talent in the kitchen from chef-owner Sébastien Leroy. The menu reads more like a combination of ingredients than recognizable dishes, but his skillful experimentation and reverence for seasonal ingredients mean that each element shines on the plate. Given a name like Sauvage (wild, untamed), it's no surprise there is a resolutely low-intervention wine list that extends to his cave à vin across the street.

22. Semilla

54, rue de Seine, 75006

Serial restaurateurs Drew Harré and Juan Sanchez have lorded over a section of Saint-Germain for years, but their elegant neo-bistro Semilla remains the standout. Seasonality is the menu's North Star, with plenty of vegetarian-friendly options and flawless wines by the glass to guide the way.

23. Sharmaji

16, rue Frémicourt, 75015

Vibrant, colorful, and full of flavor might describe chef Manoj Sharma's second restaurant (the first is Jugaad near the Opéra), a contemporary homage to

the regional Indian cooking he grew up eating. The menu highlights dishes—half of which are vegetarian—like dal with black lentils, char-grilled chicken with fennel and ginger, and pan-fried eggplant in a spicy tamarind, sesame, and yogurt sauce. The kulfi (a kind of Indian ice cream) du moment is always a sure bet, as are house-brewed beers and creative cocktails like the Indian Mule with rum, Indian masala, and vanilla (shown above).

24. La Table d'Aki

49, rue Vaneau, 75007

This elegant but compact sixteen-seater near Le Bon Marché is less of a restaurant than a collection of tables in what feels like the home kitchen of Akihiro Horikoshi, the Japanese-born chef-owner of La Table d'Aki, who does everything solo, from mise en place to cooking and baking to dishwashing. The same reverence for high-quality seafood that marked his twenty-year career at the haute temple of French fine dining, L'Ambroisie, where he was in charge of the fish course, is evident from the menu here. Dishes like lobster minestrone, squid in vegetable broth, or roasted sea bass with porcini mushrooms are simple but sophisticated, embellished by a mastery of classic French sauces.

25. Tan Dinh

60, rue de Verneuil, 75007

Opened in 1968, Tan Dinh is the oldest Vietnamese restaurant in Paris, run by two brothers who took over the operation from their mother in the late 1970s. It may seem unassuming, but locals know this is a destination for bánh cuốn-esque smoked goose ravioli that the duo pairs with rare French wines.

26. La Vera Pizza Napoletana

45, rue Brancion, 75015

It's a testament to his talents as a pizzaiolo that Guillaume Grasso draws diners to the far reaches of the 15th arrondissement while earning the approval of the Associazione Verace Pizza Napoletana for honoring Neapolitan traditions and preparations. Try the artichoke, provolone, and speck pizza or the Cosacca—a classic pie with tomato sauce, basil, and grated Pecorino Romano—and judge for yourself.

27. Ze Kitchen Galerie

4, rue des Grands Augustins, 75006

Even though it's been nearly twenty-five years since William Ledeuil first opened this singular Left Bank restaurant, it remains an incredible expression of modern French cooking. To this day, Ledeuil and his international team honor French roots but play up far-reaching influences, excelling at broths, sauces, and fish. Book for an affordable lunch or a more elaborate dinner, both featuring colorful seafood-heavy dishes that weave in bright acidity and blend Asian herbs and aromatics.

6th, 7th, 15th ARRONDISSEMENTS SHOPPING

In addition to historic cafés and broad boulevards, the neighborhoods between Saint-Germain-des-Prés and Faubourg Saint-Germain (abutting the Eiffel Tower) are known for timeless and elegant shops, like the mid-range fashion boutiques and antiques purveyors along and fanning out from the rue Bonaparte. Given the density of shoppers and travelers who find themselves behaving as flâneurs in these parts and tracing the past, it's no wonder there is an abundance of superb specialty food and home decor shops to keep them exploring. In the 6th and 7th arrondissements, there's a balanced mix of legendary icons and inventive newcomers to cover any need.

1. Alléno & Rivoire

9, rue du Champ de Mars, 75007

The first chocolate venture from acclaimed chef Yannick Alléno and his longtime pastry chef Aurélien Rivoire, this elegant boutique carries chocolates with fillings made without cream or sugar as well as candied fruits without sucrose. It's the outcome of years of research that led them to birch tree water and sap as alternatives. The total sugar content hovers around 7 percent (compared to 25 percent or more elsewhere in the industry) but doesn't compromise on taste.

2. Barthélémy

51, rue de Grenelle, 75007

A quick glance at the wall-to-wall cheese displays (on marble, bien sûr), and you'll understand why the Élysée Palace has tapped Fromagerie Barthélémy for its cheese needs since George Pompidou was president. Choose from more than two hundred types aged on-site, including superb Neufchâtels (a bloomy-rind soft cheese), mont d'or, and a robust collection of goat cheeses. But beyond those (which, you should know, will cost a pretty penny), this is the place to grab a homemade Fontainebleau, a tangy dessert made of whipped cream and faisselle (a fresh raw-milk cheese).

3. Le Café Pierre Hermé

53-57, rue de Grenelle, 75007 (Inside Beaupassage)

He's been nicknamed the Picasso of Pastry for good reason: not only is Pierre Hermé among the most talented and disruptive French pastry chefs—initiating trends and elevating the art of pastry with seasonal collections—he is the country's most successful, with boutiques all over the city and a fast-growing café brand. This one is the first, with a stunning boudoir-style interior, a full lunch menu, and all of his iconic pastries available for take-away, from the Ispahan (a mix of rose, raspberry, and lychee) in croissant or macaron form to his Infiniment collection of single-product tarts, highlighting flavors like vanilla and lemon.

4. Chapon Chocolaterie

69, rue du Bac, 75007

After making ice creams and sorbets for Buckingham Palace, Patrice Chapon turned his attention back to France and to chocolate. It's a good thing he did, or else we wouldn't have his bean-to-bar creations or the over-the-top indulgence of his chocolate mousse, scooped into a paper cone or half-pint container.

5. Chartreuse

128, boulevard Saint-Germain, 75006

Four centuries of history have led the team that distills and markets Chartreuse, the herbal liqueur developed by monks, to open a cultural center and boutique in Paris—a location chosen so they could be as close as possible to the former site of the Vauvert Carthusian monastery, which was destroyed during the French Revolution but once stood near the Luxembourg Gardens. Go to buy bottles of the "elixir of long life," along with other Alpine herbal products, but stay to learn about five hundred years of Carthusian presence in Paris.

6. Debauve & Gallais

30, rue des Saints-Pères, 75007

This is the most regal of all confectionaries. The 225-year-old historic chocolate shop, founded by Sulpice Debauve, is perhaps best known for having been the official sweets supplier to Louis XVI and the royal court at Versailles, followed by subsequent monarchs. Among the bestsellers are chocolate medallions nicknamed "pistoles de Marie Antoinette," ganaches, truffles, almond crunches, chocolate bars, and orangettes (chocolate-covered candied oranges) in elegant packaging.

7. Fromagerie Quatrehomme

62, rue de Sèvres, 75007

Quatrehomme is a name that not only signals quality, but also carries the aura of family legacy. Marie Quatrehomme, part of the second generation to run the cheese shop, won the 2000 Meilleur Ouvrier de France competition in its inaugural cheese category—and she was also the first woman to earn any MOF title since the prestigious competition's beginnings in 1925. Today, it's her adult children, Nathalie and Maxime, that run the show (and its various retail locations), but this flagship is where it all began. Pick up some of the cheeses that are aged and transformed on-site, like the Charolais goat cheese from Burgundy infused with Nikka Whisky or Camembert that's been dipped in Calvados and coated in breadcrumbs.

8. Des Gâteaux et du Pain

63, boulevard Pasteur, 75015

Claire Damon, one of Paris's most respected and wildly talented pastry chefs, has run this high-quality bakery-pâtisserie since 2006. Militant about seasonality and using only organic and biodynamic French ingredients (including almonds from Provence), Damon excels at fruit-based pastries like the pomme tatin and the Kashmir, a soft almond cake with notes of saffron, dates, and orange. There are two locations, but come to the flagship in the Montparnasse neighborhood for a wider selection.

9. La Grande Épicerie

38, rue de Sèvres, 75007

If Eataly and Union Market merged, you'd get La Grande Épicerie, the gargantuan food emporium annex of Le Bon Marché department store with one of the widest selections of wine and spirits in the city, several on-site restaurants, and deli counters. But it's also *the* go-to for gourmet snacks, fresh foods, pastry, and home goods.

10. Madame Cacao

10, rue du Cherche-Midi, 75006

After earning several top pastry titles and leading pastry at L'Élysée for three years (oui, President Macron was her boss), Christelle Brua struck out on her own with this playful chocolate shop that nods to her childhood in Alsace. You'll find puffed rice and popcorn chocolate bars, chocolate-covered marshmallow rabbits, coconut and pistachio praliné balls, and milk chocolate coated pretzels with a sprinkling of sea salt.

11. Maison Vérot

3, rue Notre Dame des Champs, 75006

Third-generation charcutier and 2011 vice-champion in the World Championship of Pâté-Croûte competition Gilles Vérot is behind this family-run fine deli known for revitalizing the pâté en croûte (see page 65). You'll find the classics, of course, but also more original recipes featuring duck and figs or kalamata olives alongside plenty of sausages, cured meats and fish, and an array of hot dishes across five Parisian retail shops.

12. Marin Montagut

48, rue Madame, 75006

It's a bit *Amélie*-meets-*Alice in Wonderland* at this multidisciplinary artist's whimsical namesake boutique across from the Luxembourg Gardens. Set in a former tapestry workshop, Montagut's shop is a portal to his playful imagination, with hand-painted homewares, travel ephemera, painted silk scarves, scented candles, and a collection of his illustrated stationery.

13. Patrick Roger
2-4, place Saint-Sulpice, 75006
The Rodin of chocolate, as the eminently artistic chocolatier Patrick Roger has been called, has a slew of boutiques across the city, but this one, in the shadow of the Saint-Sulpice church, is among the calmest. It's an ideal space to appreciate a handful of large-scale chocolate sculptures on display and ruminate on which of the immaculate fine chocolates, demi-spheres, rochers pralinés, bars, and even cooking chocolate you'll take home.

14. Poilâne
8, rue du Cherche-Midi, 75006
Bread legends were born in this location, the birthplace of Poilâne bread in 1932. The bakery, known for its tangy sourdough loaves and artistic clients like Salvador Dalí, is run today by Apollonia Poilâne, the third generation of her family to do so. She continues to experiment with ancient grains and long fermentation, turning out hundreds of thousands of addictive shortbread biscuits called punitions.

BEYOND RESTAURANTS

Coffee & Tea
Bel Horizon
Bonjour Jacob
Café du Clown
Café Nuances
Ten Belles
Terres de Café

Bars
Bar Aristide
Bar Joséphine
Le Castor Club
Grouvie
Prescription Cocktail Club
Tiger

Bread, Pâtisserie & Sweets
Arnaud Larher
Hugo & Victor
Maison le Roux
Mori Yoshida
Philippe Conticini
Pierre Hermé
Pierre Marcolini

BREAKFAST AND BRUNCH

If you can power through a morning on sweet, buttery food, the standard Parisian breakfast will appeal: a croissant or a pain au chocolat, maybe a tartine slathered with salted butter and jam, potentially a soft-boiled egg, coffee, and juice. Some variety of this sugar-laced, protein-light combination will be common across corner café menus and even on many hotel breakfast spreads. But if you want (or need) something more substantial, there are some pioneering spots around the city that have made the morning meal among the heartiest and most delicious moments to dine out.

Bob's Bake Shop
12, esplanade Nathalie Sarraute, 75018
Inspired by an American diner (but with slicker design elements), Marc Grossman's main lab and café in the 18th arrondissement turns out freshly pressed juices and specialty coffees, plump pancakes, and a variety of fresh bagels with schmear and other spreads. For a little something sweet to finish, order a slice of pie.

Café Berry
10, rue Chapon, 75003
Since 2017, eggs done every which way—soft, scrambled, Turkish, or with bacon on a bun, to name a few—have drawn fashionable crowds to this no-reservation narrow canteen in the Marais. Owner Shirley Lamy and her team serve them with excellent specialty coffee or fun alternatives (think: iced raspberry matcha or a matcha pistachio latté), buns and tea cakes, and seasonal granola bowls.

Café Méricourt
22, rue de la Folie Méricourt, 75011
An Aussie-inspired café and brunch destination, Guy Griffin's ever-popular Café Méricourt serves a balanced mix of sweet and savory dishes up until three P.M. The more unique items on the menu include a savory granola with mixed nuts, toasted oats, labneh, and marinated kale; baked eggs in a flavorful mix of spinach, leeks, onion, and pine nuts, topped with feta; orange-blossom pancakes with seasonal fruit and honey-lemon ricotta whipped cream; and a comforting congee bowl with a ramen egg.

Chiche
29, bis rue du Château d'Eau, 75010
This Israeli-inspired canteen does a mean shakshuka, challah French toast, scrambled eggs and kale with harissa mayo in a buttery croissant, and a wonderfully spicy Yemenite stew, starting at ten A.M. daily.

Echo
95, rue d'Aboukir, 75002
Matthias Gloppe's LA-inspired café (which launched in 2018 with Gjusta and Gjelina alum Mailea Weger in the kitchen) has turned locals into kale-loving, rice bowl–eating, hot sauce–curious honorary Californians. Eggs, avocado, and market greens abound, as do gluten-free and dairy-free options like pandan pancakes with berry coulis and coconut whipped

cream, and vegan shiitake bacon. If lunch fare is more your style, order the jalapeño tuna melt or Echo's signature smash burger.

L'Entente

13, rue Monsigny, 75002

This elegant British gastropub is known throughout Paris for its Sunday roasts, Scotch eggs, and Welsh rarebit, but for morning meal fans, it's a standout for weekend brunch. The menu covers the greatest hits like homemade granola, eggs Benedict, two different types of stacked pancakes, and the full English shebang: fried eggs and sausage with baked beans, mushrooms, and potatoes. A veggie-friendly version of the full English is served with plenty of greens like kale and spinach.

Hardware Société

10, rue Lamarck, 75018

With a mission to redefine breakfast and brunch for the Parisian palate, this Melbourne-born café has successfully converted locals (and plenty of visitors) to the value of the morning meal—with sweet, savory, and vegan options—since it opened in 2016. Alongside a terrific selection of specialty coffees, there are eggs or tofu cocotte, goat cheese tarts with a mushroom ragu, pulled pork buns, baked eggs and sausage, and a fruit-topped French toast.

Holybelly

5, rue Lucien Sampaix, 75010

Not only did Nicolas Alary and Sarah Mouchot put the morning meal on the Parisian map when they opened in 2013, but they have maintained the title of reigning high temple to breakfast and brunch ever since (page 105). Their success and longevity is partly a result of the menu—eggs and sides (greens, spelt hashbrowns, grilled Halloumi, or sautéed mushrooms), fluffy pancakes, chia pudding, and specials like huevos rancheros, along with premium coffee. But it might also be explained by service that goes above and beyond with a soundtrack (nineties hip-hop and rock, laughter, and plenty of "coffee up!" calls) that instantly puts diners at ease.

La Main Noire

12, rue Cavallotti, 75018

The trio of French-Australian owners of this Aussie-style café in Montmartre first created their own line of organic sticky chai (with a stickier texture than the tea most are familiar with),

and green, golden, and pink (beet and cacao) vegan pastes to incorporate into drinks or dishes that were picked up by the city's top coffee shops and épiceries. They later opened their own spot to showcase the products, which are used to make their specialty coffee drinks and teas, alongside breakfast options like chile scrambled eggs; hearty porridge; a pita toastie with mushrooms, cheese, and a fried egg; squash shakshuka; and pancakes topped with a chocolate-mascarpone whipped cream.

Maison Fleuret

30, rue des Saints-Pères, 75006

More than a very Instagrammable space, this intimate, two-story literary café housed in a nineteenth-century bookstore does brisk business for coffee, fresh juice, tea cakes, and an all-vegetarian breakfast and brunch. The portions won't sustain you for a full day of exploring the city, but dishes like a pumpkin and squash shakshuka and yogurt-almond butter bowls with granola should provide a comforting start.

P1 Bouche

151, bis rue Marcadet, 75018

This breakfast and brunch canteen from the owners of Atelier P1 bakery emerged out of recurring requests from loyal diners. Here, the menu stars are Greek or coconut yogurt granola with fresh and poached fruit; cured fish, meat, or fried eggs on house sourdough toast; and jammy soft-boiled eggs served with bread soldiers—thin strips of toast meant for dipping into the eggs.

Rose Bakery

46, bis rue des Martyrs, 75009

This is where the English-style savory breakfast really began in Paris. Two decades later, Rose Bakery on the rue des Martyrs is still a destination for scones, eggs and sides, tea cakes, veggie tarts, and top-shelf teas.

Treize au Jardin

5, rue de Médicis, 75006

This American southern-style restaurant and tearoom is known for several things: its standout location with a spacious outdoor terrace across from the Luxembourg Gardens and its all-day brunch offered until six P.M. daily. Vegetarian options abound, like the poached eggs served with a buttermilk biscuit and homemade granola bowls, but the buttermilk fried chicken has become its true calling card.

SPOTLIGHT: SANDWICHES

France has made countless celebrated contributions to the annals of gastronomy, but its sandwiches rarely get their due. Part of that has to do with culinary traditions that prize lengthy sit-down meals, but with access to superior ingredients and a deeply entrenched bread culture, Paris has a strong sandwich scene worth seeking out.

Decades after the defining falafel pita sandwiches of the rue des Rosiers and years after the burger fascination of the 2010s (which is still thriving with American-style classics at **Baby Love Burger**, smash burgers at **Dumbo**, and bistro iterations at **PNY**, **Blend**, **Le Ruisseau**, and **Bomaye**), sandwich culture has taken over the street food scene. Not only is le sandwich among the fastest- growing categories, but it is the one that generates the most fervent enthusiasm among consumers.

"What we're seeing now is a course correction on quite an anomaly," says food entrepreneur Julien Pham. "Even if the jambon-beurre is one of the greatest symbols of French gastronomy, and the bánh mì our earliest example of a made-to-order sandwich, Parisians have had very limited access to quality sandwiches—what's sold in bakeries is often soggy, made with low-cost ingredients and advanced preparation, sometimes even the night before."

Thoughtful sandwich makers have moved the format into the realm of cuisine—something with value that should be considered more than a grab-and-go import. Look for international deli sandwiches at **Le Favori** (try Le Tunisien with tuna, peppers, egg, capers, olives, and harissa on a Mamiche-made bun), fluffy Japanese sandos at **Benchy** or **Carré Pain de Mie**, the sabich (an Iraqi fried eggplant pita sandwich) at **La Sabicherie**, arayes (Middle Eastern stuffed pita sandwiches) and laffa wrapped sandwich on a homemade naan-like bread with grilled chicken and amba sauce (fermented mango with curry) at **Nour Comptoir**, spicy fried chicken sandwiches, American or Korean style, on brioche buns or biscuits at **Buck**, **Dogma**, and **Krispy**, gourmet kebabs at **Gemüse** and **Mehmet** (page 151), and fancy baguette sandwiches at **Olga**.

Part of this shift came as a result of the global reach of social media and the affordability of travel. Mina Soundiram, a food journalist for Brut and the television show *Très Très Bon* who has covered street food for nearly fifteen years, points to the ease with which consumers and food entrepreneurs can spend time everywhere from Los Angeles to Hanoi and bring back notions of the local street food culture. "Street food, and sandwiches in particular, travel well. They're a way to understand other cultures. What's more, they're affordable, and they fit within the changing norms of the French lunch break, which is far shorter than the two-hour pause it once was." Those who can't spontaneously travel only have to pick up their devices and tap into a world of sandwich inspiration stemming from all corners of the globe.

Pham argues there's yet a third factor—the coffee shop. "What helped was also the advent of a new type of place for Paris. The specialty coffee shop didn't only offer good coffee but a simple lunch that included sandwiches. Those who couldn't find what they were looking for in bakeries could sit down for a quiet lunch with a truly good sandwich made fresh."

While eat-on-the-go culture has its roots in the United States, the sandwich's influences are far more wide-reaching—found all over South America, Turkey, and the Middle East—and it is that diversity that is rapidly shaping the tastes of the Parisian palate.

Baby Love Burger
63, rue Saint-Maur, 75011

Dumbo
Multiple locations

PNY
Multiple locations

Blend
Multiple locations

Le Ruisseau
22, rue Rambuteau, 75003

Bomaye
10, rue de Paradis, 75010

Le Favori
112, rue Saint-Maur, 75011

Benchy
50, rue du Cherche-Midi, 75006

Carré Pain de Mie
5, rue Rambuteau, 75004

La Sabicherie
33, rue du Faubourg Saint-Antoine, 75011

Nour Comptoir
38, rue Jean-Pierre Timbaud, 75011

Buck
25, rue de la Forge Royale, 75011

Dogma
10, rue des Petites Écuries, 75010

Krispy
22, rue Biot, 75017

Gemüse
61, rue Ramey, 75018

Olga
3, rue Michel Chasles, 75012

Le jambon-beurre

If there is one quintessentially Parisian sandwich, it's le jambon-beurre. Nicknamed "le parisien," this ham-and-butter classic is a three-ingredient staple that rose to prominence as the preferred lunch of choice among workers at Les Halles central food market in the second half of the nineteenth century. Back then, le parisien was simply two slices of rustic country bread smeared with lard. It soared in popularity in the 1930s before shapeshifting twenty years later into the sandwich we know today. The demi-baguette, split length-wise, replaced the country bread and became the gold standard for the ham sandwich. The bread is slathered on both sides with butter (salted or unsalted, depending on where you go), then filled gener-ously with ham or pâté. Purists know this doesn't include just any ham, it should be Paris ham (jambon

Prince de Paris), two thin strips en chiffonade, to be precise. And it should be sandwiched between a baguette tradition (see page 63). The final touch: a sizable, crunchy cornichon or two, sliced lengthwise.

Each of the city's top jambon-beurre may vary slightly according to venue: at **Caractère de Cochon** in the Marais, you have a choice between cured ham (Noir de Bigorre) or boiled ham and the addition of cheese—Saint-Nectaire, Ossau-Iraty, or aged Comté. At **Le Petit Vendôme**, around the corner from the place Vendôme's swanky jewelry stores, you'll find the crisp demi-baguette spread with unsalted butter and stuffed with ham cooked on the bone—cornichon optional. Meanwhile, **CheZaline**, a beloved sliver of a sandwich shop in the 11th arrondissement originally founded by Delphine Zampetti, goes about them more simply: Prince de Paris ham and demi-sel butter, that's it. Don't dare ask for cornichons.

Caractère de Cochon
2, rue Charlot, 75003

Le Petit Vendôme
8, rue des Capucines, 75002

CheZaline
85, rue de la Roquette, 75011

The American way

We must give credit where it is unquestionably due: American culture has significantly influenced Paris's booming sandwich scene. Some of the most enduring shops in the city have been launched by Americans themselves, like Orly Zeitoun, who makes mouth-stretching veggie and pulled pork sandwiches jazzed up with homemade condiments at her 9th arrondissement shop **Snack Attack,** and Marc Grossman with his housemade bagel sandwiches at **Shakespeare and Company Café** (page 49), and **Bob's Bake Shop** (page 84) that could rival any of the New York City icons. But the most buzzworthy bites have come from the minds of French Americanophiles who have spent lengthy periods of time traveling and researching food culture in the United States.

Jean Ganizate and Paul Loiseleur discovered Texas barbecue in 2012 while interning in the US and saw the potential for broad success in Paris, where regional American staples were finding a welcome audience. They traversed the Barbecue Belt, *Texas Monthly*'s selection of the state's very best, met pitmaster Jeffrey Howard of Dallas's Pecan Lodge, and convinced him to move to Paris to help them launch **Melt**, which first opened in 2016. Three restaurants and two delis later, and their slow-smoked brisket, pulled pork, spareribs, pork belly, and lamb ribs are still drawing in crowds.

Matthias Gloppe first made his mark with **Echo** (page 84) but followed in early 2024 with **Kiss**, a California-inspired take-away shop designed by US-based creative director Anna Polonsky with a clever sandwich menu developed by Peter Lemos of Wax Paper in Los Angeles. In the morning, he serves Tex-Mex breakfast tacos and egg sandwiches on an English muffin but ramps up the offerings at lunch with recipes like The GodMother, where mortadella and prosciutto is loaded up with red onions, shredded pecorino, and spicy sauce on soft sesame bread; the Veggies Trippin, which combines turnip kohlrabi, yellow beets, apple, and shredded cheddar on a honey-butter-slathered baguette; or the Turkey Supper Club, which layers sliced roasted turkey, provolone, pickled jalapeños, and coleslaw on ciabatta.

But the biggest success story of all began with a lobster roll experiment at a **Le Food Market** (page 173) pop-up, prepared by then twenty-one-year-old entrepreneur Moïse Sfez and sold at a loss, that would become the calling card of his Homer Food Group. Sfez discovered the lobster roll as a teen visiting the US and returned to France obsessed and committed to the idea of incorporating the sandwich into his own venture. Hospitality school followed, then stints in Michelin kitchens in Paris before he tested his own take on the New England classic. The recipe that regularly sells out at his various locations across Paris of **Homer Lobster** and won him the Celebrity Pick at the 2018 *Down East Magazine* World's Best Lobster Roll Competition (the only European to have entered the competition), is made on homemade toasted brioche and topped with lobster, homemade mayonnaise, and chives. In preparation, the whole lobster is blanched, shelled, and cooked sous-vide at medium temperature before being cut up and weighed just before service begins.

When it came to the next project in his growing empire, Sfez drew inspiration from S&P Lunch, his favorite NYC sandwich shop. **Janet**, his more affordable shop named after his late grandmother, is designed like a modernist deli with counter seats and a sleek bar gantry, and serves a tight menu of tuna melts, corned beef and pastrami on homemade rye, house-smoked turkey, slow-cooked beef BBQ, and his surprise bestseller, the triple decker club sandwich. Packed at lunch and dinner, it isn't uncommon to see chefs from top restaurants dining alongside local sandwich groupies. He followed this success in 2024 with **Maurice Café**, a coffee bar with egg and cheese on house-made English muffins and Liège waffles (because, why not?).

Snack Attack
27, rue Marguerite de Rochechouart, 75009

Melt
Multiple locations

Kiss
55, rue du Faubourg Poissonnière, 75009

Homer Lobster
Multiple locations

Janet
13, rue Rambuteau, 75004

Maurice Café
14, rue Rambuteau, 75004

Le bánh mì

One of the most iconic and beloved dishes in Paris, the Vietnamese bánh mì is sold everywhere from the city's oldest Chinatown in the 3rd arrondissement to the contemporary Chinatowns in the 13th arrondissement and the northern district of Belleville. Baguettes were introduced into Vietnam during the French colonial occupation in the nineteenth century, and soon after, the sandwich found a lasting global dining audience. In Vietnam, it's the street food dish on every corner, usually set up in small mobile stands. According to chef Khánh-Ly Huynh, who co-owns **The Hood** (page 105) and **Nonette**, a bánh mì and doughnut shop in the 11th arrondissement, the Parisian iteration of the sandwich rarely features top-quality bread or ingredients that have been cured or pickled in-house—which is part of why the sandwich has historically been so inexpensive. That's not the case at her establishments nor **Miss Banh Mi**, **Hanoï Corner**, and **Bánh mì 13**, where the specialty gets the utmost care and attention.

Nonette
71, rue Jean-Pierre Timbaud, 75011

Miss Banh Mi
5, rue Mandar, 75002

Hanoï Corner
7, rue Blanche, 75009

Bánh mì 13
66, avenue d'Ivry, 75013

HOTELS FOR FOOD LOVERS

Some of the most inventive and exciting dining experiences can be found within the sharply designed interiors of the city's best hotels. That is particularly true for temples of fine dining, such as Plénitude and Le Cinq, which are both highlights of two iconic properties. And while these tables can be challenging to book, snagging a reservation tends to be slightly easier if you're a guest of the hotel. If that isn't in the cards, fret not: there is plenty of affordable win-ing and dining to be had elsewhere.

Le Bar Long at Le Royal Monceau — Raffles Paris

37, avenue Hoche, 75008

If you're into hotel bars and fortified wines, make a stop for an apéritif or a nightcap at the Philippe Starck–designed Le Bar Long. It's one of the few bars in Paris to offer an extensive selection of port wines from three major houses—Fonseca, Quinta do Noval, and Taylor's—and a range of styles, carefully selected by the hotel's head sommelier.

Boubalé at Le Grand Mazarin Hotel

6, rue des Archives, 75004

It's a fairly bold choice to have semi-fine-dining Ashkenazi Jewish cooking anchor a high-end hotel—the cuisine is one that's drastically underrepresented in Paris. But the acclaimed Jerusalem-born chef Assaf Granit of **Shabour** (page 18) draws from his Polish and German grandmothers' home-cooking repertoire with great finesse, serving dishes like yellowtail ceviche in a horseradish marinade; chopped chicken liver ("gehackte leber"), presented in a large spoon with egg powder, caramelized onions, black pepper, croutons, and gherkins; plump kreplach (dumplings) stuffed with beef cheek, paprika, Parmesan, and almonds; and a Jewish chicken soup twist on the Palestinian musakhan. The wines are similarly diverse for Paris, with bottles from Slovenia, Hungary, Romania, and Armenia. Request a counter seat to watch the meal unfold in the open kitchen.

Le Cinq and Le George at the Four Seasons George V

31, avenue George V, 75008

After more than ten years at the helm of the Four Seasons George V's three-Michelin-starred restaurant Le Cinq, chef Christian Le Squer has managed to maintain both its relevance and its staying power with his cooking, which follows French tradition in concept but is fully contemporary on the plate. And if French isn't speaking to you but the George V universe is, an exceptionally good second option is chef Simone Zanoni's Mediterranean menu (with set or à la carte options) at Le George. Fresh pastas, fish, and plenty of vegetarian options (like the outstanding candied tomato tarte tatin with cacio e pepe ice cream) abound, and the chef will cook an all-vegan menu upon request for the entire table.

Citrons et Huîtres at Hôtel Rochechouart

57, boulevard Marguerite de Rochechouart, 75009

The spirit of the roaring twenties is alive and well at this south Pigalle boutique hotel. There's a warm-weather rooftop bar that nearly puts the Sacré Coeur within arm's reach and a sprawling brasserie, as well as nightclub Mikado Dancing, open Friday and Saturday nights. But the more contemporary standout is Citrons et Hûitres, an adjoining seafood crudo bar named after the painting of the same name by Renoir, whose last studio was located in the same building. You'll gather around a central stainless-steel counter to throw back Brittany oysters, fish rillettes, and shrimp tartines, with sparkling wine at the ready.

Espadon at the Ritz Paris

15, place Vendôme, 75001

This post-Covid renaissance of the legendary Espadon (formerly with an *L'*) at the Ritz Paris hotel takes over a banquet room where Charles Ritz had originally set up the restaurant in 1956. Now it's done up in warm tones and has a crystal glass roof and striking semi-open kitchen framed in copper. Chef Eugénie Béziat is the first woman to lead the kitchen here, and she rightfully brings a fresh, new style to the destination, complete with clever touches that draw from her upbringing in Gabon, the Congo, and the Ivory Coast, like grilled lobster tail served in a jus of bissap.

Fouquet's at the Hôtel Barrière Le Fouquet's

99, avenue des Champs-Élysées, 75008

With its prime location on the corner of avenue George V and avenue des Champs-Élysées and a long history hosting luminaries from Charlie Chaplin and Liza Minnelli to Bradley Cooper, this brasserie has cemented itself into the annals of Parisian dining lore. Opened in 1899, Fouquet's is the place to see and be seen (and hopefully catch an exciting sighting or two) and also happens to have a stellar chef attached to it: Pierre Gagnaire oversees the seasonal menu.

Le Gabriel at La Réserve

42, avenue Gabriel, 75008

A three-starred jewel of a restaurant helmed by chef Jérôme Banctel inside La Réserve hotel (page 130).

Jacques' Bar at The Hoxton

30-32, rue du Sentier, 75002

True to its intention, The Hoxton's Paris location is an all-day destination. Locals and travelers linger for hours beneath the hotel's glass-canopied central courtyard, sipping coffee and cocktails. But for a more intimate bar experience, head up a spiral staircase (one of many original features from the eighteenth century) to reach Jacques' Bar, where the sequence of drinks on the craft cocktail menu—Foreplay, Let's Get It On, and For a Nightcap—set the evening's tone.

Nonos & Comestibles at Hôtel de Crillon

6, rue Boissy d'Anglas, 75008

After he spent more than twenty years cooking in Shanghai, Paul Pairet's return to Europe brought him to the Hôtel de Crillon, a Rosewood Hotel, where he leads this sleek modern steakhouse and snack bar (page 131).

Plénitude at the Cheval Blanc Paris

8, quai du Louvre, 75001

Arnaud Donckele is not only one of France's kindest chefs; he's among the fastest rising stars in the industry. After landing three stars for La Vague d'Or at the Cheval Blanc hotel in Saint-Tropez, he brings the same creative sensibility, complexity, and obsession with sauces—which are the starting point for developing each dish—to this twenty-six-seater at Cheval Blanc Paris. Handling plated desserts is Maxime Frédéric, the other megawatt star of Cheval Blanc, whose supreme talents with pastry earned him a spot across the street creating exclusive desserts for the Louis Vuitton café. Here's the catch: With three stars and so few covers, there's at least a year's wait for a table at Plénitude (the maître d'hôtel tries to prioritize hotel guests, if that's an option). Luckily, the duo also oversees the property's Japanese restaurant, Hakuba, and its upscale brasserie, Le Tout Paris, which boasts similarly spectacular Seine-side views.

Shang Palace at Shangri-La

10, avenue d'Iéna, 75016

As France's first and only Chinese restaurant to be awarded a Michelin star, Shang Palace is an ideal spot to experience the elegance and diversity of Cantonese cooking and how it intersects with more local French influences. The meal unfurls inside the historic surroundings of the Shangri-La Hotel, which occupies a nineteenth-century private mansion that was once owned by descendants of Napoleon I.

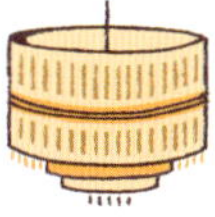

Canal Saint-Martin
Faubourg-Poissonnière
Gare du Nord
Marché d'Aligre
Oberkampf

10th, 11
ARRONDI

4

th, 12th
SEMENTS

DINING

1. Le 52 Faubourg Saint-Denis
2. Les Arlots
3. Åke
4. Aux Deux Amis
5. Le Bistrot Paul Bert
6. Bouche
7. BMK Folie-Bamako
8. La Brigade du Tigre
9. Brutos
10. Café les Deux Gares
11. Café du Coin
12. Le Chardenoux
13. Le Châteaubriand
14. Clamato
15. Comer
16. Le Comptoir Sur Mer
17. Delhi Bazaar
18. Early June
19. Eels
20. Furia
21. Gramme 11
22. Gros Bao
23. Ground Control
24. Haikara
25. Holybelly
26. The Hood
27. Jah Jah
28. Kubri
29. Maison
30. Mansouria
31. Mokonuts
32. Oobatz
33. Özlem
34. Passerini
35. Pierre Sang
36. Le Repaire de Cartouche
37. Reyna
38. Le Rigmarole
39. Le Saint Sébastien
40. Septime
41. Le Servan
42. Le Tagine
43. Taverna
44. La Taverne de Zhao
45. Le Train Bleu
46. Urfa Dürüm
47. Le Verre Volé
48. Waly-Fay

10th, 11th, 12th ARRONDISSEMENTS

SHOPPING

1. AXS Design
2. La Bague de Kenza
3. Buddy Buddy
4. Chambelland
5. Chambre Noire
6. Le Chocolat Alain Ducasse-Manufacture
7. La Compagnie du Mieux Boire
8. Confiture Parisienne
9. Delicatessen Cave
10. Folderol
11. JJ Hings
12. Julhès
13. Landline
14. Liquiderie Cave
15. Mamiche
16. Marché d'Aligre
17. Olga
18. Taka & Vermo
19. Ten Belles Bread
20. Utopie

10th, 11th, 12th ARRONDISSEMENTS DINING

The neighborhoods on the northern edge of République and east toward place de la Nation are among the city's most popular when it comes to contemporary dining in Paris. This is not necessarily white-tablecloth and black-bow-tie-wearing-waiter territory, but rather, the area where you'll find exposed stone walls, minimalist decor, and international chefs earning buzz for their affordable seasonal cuisine, beloved by Veja-wearing bohemians.

This zone encompasses place de la République, which is the city's largest pedestrian square in Paris and iconic for its bronze statue of Marianne, the national symbol of freedom, at its center. It's also a rallying point for protests, demonstrations, and public gatherings and at the junction of three popular arrondissements: the 3rd, 10th, and 11th.

Off of nearby rue de Château d'Eau, all along rue du Faubourg Saint-Denis, and on both sides of the boulevard de Magenta, you'll find a cross-culture of populations and some of the city's top bakeries, craft coffee shops, and sought-after neo-bistros and natural wine bars. You could say it's where each of those movements truly blossomed in France, with spots like Le Verre Volé, Du Pain et des Idées, and Ten Belles leading the charge.

To the north sit two of the city's major transportation hubs: Gare de l'Est, constructed in 1849 to service destinations east of the city, and Gare du Nord, built in 1863 and known for its Eurostar journeys across the Channel.

Further east is rue Oberkampf and rue de Charonne in the 11th arrondissement, both chock-full of independently run épiceries, wine shops, and sourdough-slinging bakeries. At night, tables in these parts book out weeks, if not months, in advance with tasting menus and pop-up residencies hosted by world-renowned chefs.

With the exception of the Coulée Verte (or Promenade Plantée)—Paris's very own elevated walkway, which inspired New York's High Line—there are few tourist sites or attractions on this side of town. There's the July Column at the heart of the place de la Bastille, commemorating the revolution of 1830, as well as the modern Opéra Bastille, but the next big destination sits further down in the 12th arrondissement. That's where you'll find the outdoor Marché d'Aligre, a vibrant produce market open six days a week, with more than enough shops, restaurants, and bars nearby to fill an itinerary.

1. Le 52 Faubourg Saint-Denis

52, rue du Faubourg Saint-Denis, 75010

Charles Compagnon's pioneering neo-brasserie (a few blocks from his other star project, Le Richer) remains an all-day draw for Right Bank locals who have come to expect an inventive and ever-changing seasonal menu at lunch and dinner (always with a vegetarian option), house-roasted coffee, and a wide selection of eaux-de-vie.

2. Les Arlots

136, rue du Faubourg Poissonnière, 75010

It may look like a hundred other Parisian bistros, with wooden chairs, worn floor tiles, and a short chalkboard menu of deceivingly simple-sounding dishes. But that's where the similarity ends: Les Arlots soars above the rest with its execution, particularly when it comes to the herby saucisse-purée drizzled with jus. It's done with a pan-fried pork sausage made in-house and generous mashed potatoes that contain more butter than perhaps you'd care to know.

3. Åke

8, rue Marie et Louise, 75010

In this wooden-chic neo-bistro a block from the Canal Saint-Martin, the Swedish-born chef Linda Granebring delivers simple, seasonal shared plates from a compact open kitchen. The menu is tight (consider ordering one of everything) but always includes a golden gnocchi dish, a couple of meat and fish options, cheese, and some variation on the pavlova (her calling card) for dessert. Leave drinks up to the sommelier and co-owner, Julien Jack Alda, who knows what low-intervention wines or sakés pair best with each plate.

4. Aux Deux Amis

45, rue Oberkampf, 75011

This is the kind of bustling, classically Parisian natural wine bar that has inspired New York's and London's own iterations. But no international replica comes close to the relaxed energy, accessibility (inexpensive wine and small plates), design (yellow tables and fluorescent lighting), and selection that have made David Loyola's lunch, apéro, and dinner spot a mainstay.

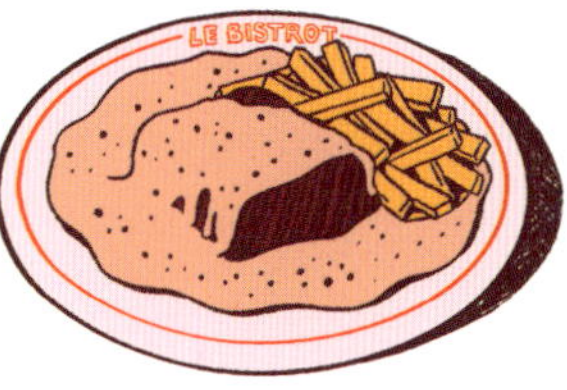

5. Le Bistrot Paul Bert

18, rue Paul Bert, 75011

If any gut-busting bistro has come to typify the star power of the 11th arrondissement (and draw in diners from far-reaching neighborhoods), it's Bertrand Auboyneau's legendary Bistrot Paul Bert. Come hungry for archetypal classics like côte de boeuf for two (medium-rare only), steak au poivre, sole meunière, perfectly salted fries, and textbook soufflé. As with most bistro relics, reservations are taken only by phone, or you can walk in. If it's full, go next door to L'Ecailler du Bistrot, a seafood annex founded and run by Auboyneau's wife, Gwénaëlle Cadoret, which serves the Rolls-Royce of oysters sourced directly from her family's production in Brittany.

6. Bouche

85, rue Jean-Pierre Timbaud, 75011

If you like the idea of dining by candlelight, discovering a tightly edited list of minimal-intervention wines, and digging into a slew of Southeast Asian–inspired small plates with your friends, Bouche is a neighborhood star. Go at night or book midday on Sunday, when the menu leans un peu brunchy. If you can't get in, head across the square to the team's wine and slice shop, Rori.

7. BMK Folie-Bamako

40, rue Jean-Pierre Timbaud, 75011

The second of Fousseyni Djikine's family-run Malian canteens, this peachy-hued BMK outpost is a hit at lunch and dinner for Malian and Pan-African comforts and bissap, a chilled hibiscus tea. There's mafe inspired by a family recipe, a stew prepared with fresh peanuts grilled over a wood fire and immersed in a creamy sauce simmered with smoked chicken; zaamé, the Malian version of Senegalese thiep, combining French beef and Penja pepper; and a handful of hearty vegan stews.

8. La Brigade du Tigre

38, rue du Faubourg Poissonnière, 75010

"Fusion" may still be a tricky word, but chef Adrien Ferrand (who also owns Eels) and Galien Emery strike a smart balance here, mastering spice and other flavors they fell in love with while traveling through China, Malaysia, Cambodia, and Thailand. Awarded a Michelin Bib Gourmand, the result comes together in a bistro setting with dishes meant for sharing: crispy pork ravioli, eggplant sushi, and black sesame baos.

9. Brutos

5, rue du Général Renault, 75011

Looking out onto the pedestrian-only Square Gardette, Brutos is a Brazilian grill–meets–Parisian neo-bistro bathed in golden light. Ninon Lecomte and her chef-husband, Lucas Baur de Campos, who trained with Joël Robuchon, grill, braise, and roast it all over an open flame, from aged beefsteaks, prime ribs, morcilla, blood sausage, fish, and whole chicken (which is the focus of the Sunday lunch menu). Go for the garlicky fries and the sleeper hit side, farofa, a Brazilian toasted manioc flour dish commonly served with meat. Stick with the French-dominant natural wines during the meal and then head two doors down to the couple's watering hole, Bar Principal, for inventive cocktails. Should hunger strike again, try one of the outstanding bar snacks like a mushroom croque monsieur, homemade chicken terrine, and fried tapioca cubes with guava dipping sauce.

10. Café les Deux Gares

1, rue des Deux Gares, 75010

Perched between two train stations, the Gare de l'Est and the Gare du Nord, and overlooking the tracks, the Café des Deux Gares has an old-timey aesthetic from the British designer Luke Edward Hall and a contemporary bistro focus by chef Jonathan Schweizer. The meat- and seafood-heavy dishes are generous and sophisticated both at lunch and dinner, rightfully earning a crew of regulars.

11. Café du Coin

9, rue Camille Desmoulins, 75011

A few blocks from the Père Lachaise cemetery, the Café du Coin is both literally a café on a corner and the quintessential neighborhood all-day café. The serial restaurateur Florent Ciccoli (of Jones, Recoin, and L'Orillon Bar, all in the 11th arrondissement and each worth your time) has mastered the simple-is-best principle of good dining with dishes like gremolata ravioli in a bath of tomato water, seasonal pizzettes, and

comforting desserts. Funky wine and specialty coffee make natural companions.

12. Le Chardenoux
1, rue Jules Vallès, 75011
Where the nearby Bistrot Paul Bert is rustic, Le Chardenoux is opulent, full of original Art Nouveau details (ornate moldings and cornices, frosted glass, and a prominent zinc bar). Taken over by France's most beloved celebrity chef Cyril Lignac in 2014, the menu is heavily fish-focused but has a stellar burger (shown above) and the chef's bestselling baba au rhum for dessert—also sold at his pastry shop across the street.

13. Le Châteaubriand
129, avenue Parmentier, 75011
Basque chef Iñaki Aizpitarte's Le Châteaubriand has been a bastion of the bistronomy movement since it opened eighteen years ago. Little has changed in that time, not the 1930s-era interiors, the casual service, nor the set, no-choice menu that plays up unexpected flavor pairings and textures. An ideal spot for diners looking to be surprised.

14. Clamato
80, rue de Charonne, 75011
Septime's seafood-focused little sister, located next door, is a hit for two big reasons: Locals love its natural wines by the glass and small plates of marinated fish, oysters, and more unusual-for-Paris dishes like shrimp lettuce cups with satay sauce as much as they love the fact that it's open on Sunday—one of few in the area. Walk-ins only; don't leave without trying the signature Clamatarte—a maple syrup tartelette topped with vanilla whipped cream.

15. Comer
96, rue d'Hauteville, 75010
There's no better place in Paris for contemporary Mexican food than chef Carlos Moreno's bright and airy café in the 10th arrondissement. Using traditional techniques and seasonal French ingredients, the menu is based around regional recipes—including some from his native Tabasco. That may translate to albóndigas al chipotle, encacahuatados (enchiladas often with mushrooms in a creamy mole sauce with peanuts and smoked pepper), and huarache, corn tortillas topped with shredded pork, black beans, and a garnish of fresh herbs. Save room for the de elote, a fresh cornbread cake that he serves alongside coconut yogurt mousse drizzled with cajeta (goat milk caramel) and toasted almonds.

16. Le Comptoir Sur Mer
53, rue de Lancry, 75010
Set on a food-centric street located a few blocks from

the Canal Saint-Martin, Le Comptoir Sur Mer is one of the city's best places to find fish and seafood. The Belgian-Ugandan chef-owner, Olive Davoux, brings in sustainably sourced oysters, clams, mussels, sardines, and tuna from small fishermen for her heaping platters (shown on page 103) and briny dishes gussied up with homemade teriyaki, Bordier butter with nori seaweed, or the nam jim sauce that changes daily. Unsurprisingly, the drink of choice here is one of the minimal-intervention wines in a similar vein to the selections down the street at Le Verre Volé. For heartier seafood dishes and all-day service, head to the chef's annex two blocks away at 1, rue de Marseille.

17. Delhi Bazaar

71, rue Servan, 75011

This slick, Dishoom-inspired spot with decorative nods to New Delhi fills a gap in the 11th arrondissement, where neo-bistros abound but Indian cuisine has been all but absent. Sip on a spiced cocktail and order a few dishes from each menu category: the chaats (don't skip the dahi puri, shown below left), the tandooris, and the classics, dotted with curries and biryanis to share. Save room for desserts like the cardamom kulfi sundae, an ice cream dessert, and Shahi Tukra, billed as an Indian French toast.

18. Early June

19, rue Jean Poulmarch, 75010

It's first come, first served for parties fewer than four at this rustic-chic natural wine bar off the Canal Saint-Martin. Part of what makes it so popular and compelling is its rotating cast of guest chefs from around the world who stay anywhere from a week to a few months to cook, introducing locals to an incredible range of flavors and styles. Check Early June's Instagram for the upcoming residencies.

19. Eels

27, rue d'Hauteville, 75010

One of the most innovative neo-bistros in a neighborhood teeming with them, Eels has been consistently impressive since it opened in 2017. Chef Adrien Ferrand's spirited and highly technical dishes are ever-changing but will invariably include the house signature smoked eel starter—perhaps with a kiwi and almond sauce, a crunchy crumble with tangy sorrel leaves—and other vegetable-forward recipes that make abundant use of herbs, citrus, Asian ingredients, and a variety of textures.

20. Furia

2, rue Lacharrière, 75011

At Furia, Julio Guerrero and Oliver Lomeli (of Chambre Noire) offer their take on a Mexican taqueria within a Parisian neo-bistro, tastefully combining excellent meat and veggie tacos, tostadas, and pickled snacks to nibble on with French and German natural wines.

21. Gramme 11

96, rue Jean-Pierre Timbaud, 75011

This café–meets–wine bar, from the same owners as the tiny canteen of the same name in the Marais, is open for apéro and dinner, with a reliably hip crowd of natural wine lovers who flock here for seasonal dishes inflected with Southeast Asian flavors. The one menu mainstay worth ordering is the Vietnamese chou farci—stuffed cabbage with pork and shrimp, served in a shrimp bouillon.

22. Gros Bao

72, quai de Jemmapes, 75010

This two-story Chinese canteen from the Bao Family restaurant group

is among the most high-energy and well-designed highlights along the Canal Saint-Martin. You'll find made-to-order bao, creative cocktails, shareable plates (the eggplant in soy sauce and the fresh noodle salad are excellent), and mood-setting design—Formica tables from Hong Kong, bright red waxed concrete floors, and red hanging lamps—meant to lend a playful feel.

23. Ground Control

81, rue du Charolais, 75012

This cultural space–meets–food hall set up in a disused rail depot is a genuinely fun spot to hang out. You'll find various food trucks outdoors and wine, craft beers, and cocktails on the inside, along with an organic food market and The Refugee Food association's permanent restaurant La Résidence. Go to eat and stay for one of the many weekly cultural and culinary events.

24. Haikara

82, rue de la Folie Méricourt, 75011

Chef Sho Miyashita's brick-walled izakaya looks unassuming but delivers some of the best small plates in the neighborhood. Lunch consists of four different types of donburi with sides like miso-broiled eggplant topped with katsuobushi (bonito flakes) or banbanji (sesame sauce). Dinner goes full tapas with duck tataki in ponzu sauce, okonomiyaki (a grilled cabbage pancake), and sashimi, alongside two cocktail options on tap, saké, and natural wines. For comfort food, head to the chef's second spot, Haikara Deep Fried, a ten-minute walk away.

25. Holybelly

5, rue Lucien Sampaix, 75010

What started as a coffee shop didn't remain one for long: Holybelly quickly evolved into a full-fledged restaurant with a savory all-day breakfast menu that easily rivals the best American and Aussie brunches. Think: excellent specialty coffee, hearty egg dishes, granola and chia pudding, and the fluffiest pancakes in the city. There are also daily specials, a rotating selection of desserts, and remarkably attentive service.

26. The Hood

80, rue Jean-Pierre Timbaud, 75011

Singaporean food was noticeably absent from the Parisian food scene until Pearlyn Lee opened The Hood in 2016, blending specialty coffee, natural wines, and dishes like Hainanese chicken rice, kaya toast, sambal stingray, chili crab and mantou, and pandan cake (plus other hawker classics and a host of vegetarian and vegan options), all served with housemade condiments. If you're in the mood for something quicker, head across the street to Nonette, Lee's bánh mì counter, for sandwiches on fresh bread with house-made charcuterie and house-pickled vegetables.

27. Jah Jah

11, rue des Petites Écuries, 75010

Jah Jah isn't merely a colorful, Rasta-inspired Afro-vegan canteen: The owners, Coralie Jouhier and Daquisiline Gomis, regularly organize reggae nights (look out for Jah Jah Sound System alerts on Instagram) that keep the community well-fed *and* entertained.

28. Kubri

108, rue Amelot, 75011

What does creative contemporary Lebanese dining look like? Kubri, with its bright menu by executive chef Rita Higgins that celebrates the flavors of the Levant while also drawing from her years working in Japan. Mezze and family-style mains change seasonally, but you'll always find several hummus dishes (if offered, order the iteration with poached egg and shimeji, small Japanese mushrooms); lamb chops with stuffed grape leaves and labneh; and a melt-in-your-mouth shawarma côte de boeuf meant for sharing. Don't skip out on the cocktails.

29. Maison

3, rue Saint-Hubert, 75011

Eastern Paris's most unique dining experience unfurls at Maison, the aptly named private home, complete with terra-cotta tiles on a gable roof, that doubles as the first solo restaurant from the Tokyo-born chef Sota Atsumi. He first gained attention for creative takes on traditional French dishes like sweetbreads, brains, and pithiviers de canard, a duck-filled pie made of puff pastry, when he was cooking at Clown Bar. Here, those may make appearances (especially during game season), but the chef's no-choice tasting menu, prepared from an open loft-style kitchen on the mezzanine floor, is dictated only by the market and his whims. If budget allows, opt for the wine pairing for a truly memorable meal.

30. Mansouria

11, rue Faidherbe, 75011

Fatéma Hal not only opened this wonderful temple to couscous in 1984, but also wrote *the* book on the topic—exploring the origins of the dish through 150 recipes. A small selection of those recipes and regional variants makes its way onto the menu at this chic Moroccan bistro, in addition to other signatures like the pigeon pastilla and the mrouzia, a lamb tagine with raisins, almonds, and honey with origins in the twelfth century.

31. Mokonuts

5, rue Saint-Bernard, 75011

It's a testament to their tremendous cooking and popularity that the Japanese-Lebanese duo behind Mokonuts, Moko Hirayama and Omar Koreitem, only open on weekdays. The couple insists their intimate operation escapes any neat definition, but you'll find the best of French meat, fish, and produce combined with Middle Eastern inflections, along with the best cookies in town. For breakfast or all-day snacks, head a few doors down to their café Mokochaya, and for dinner service, go to nearby Mokoloco, the couple's chef-in-residence sister restaurant.

32. Oobatz

4, bis avenue Jean Aicard, 75011

The American sourdough baker Dan Pearson first earned attention for his sold-out pizza pop-ups at Le Rigmarole, run under the name Pizzamarole. It was the perfect training ground for Oobatz (Italian American for "crazy"), his first solo home for his specialty pies. You'll find six sourdough pizzas that change regularly but always include a margherita and might range from polpette (meatball) and caciocavallo cheese to endive, bleu de chèvre, and scamorza. Cult-favorite desserts from the pop-up maintain their starring role at the end of the meal, like the pizzookie, a jumbo-sized chocolate chip cookie served hot with vanilla ice cream, and a cinnamon-apple crumble and cheesecake ice cream. Order a bottle of natural wine for the table, or have a glass of Pearson's favorite craft beer on tap from Basqueland. Walk-ins accepted at the counter.

33. Özlem

57, rue des Petites Écuries, 75010

Of all the top kebab spots in Paris, this is likely the only one to eschew fries in favor of rice, wheat, or vegetables. Other things the owner Edip Bolatoglu feels strongly about: making everything in-house, including the tomato-based sauce with a touch of harissa, and using the highest-quality meat possible. Order a glass of ayran, a salty and frothy Turkish yogurt drink, to go with your kebab.

34. Passerini

65, rue Traversière, 75012

Ever since the Roman chef Giovanni Passerini started cooking in Paris, he's filled the culinary gap between Italian classics and fine dining, with a highly personal, contemporary bistro style of cooking. À la carte, you'll find fresh pasta (also sold at his adjacent shop Pastificio Passerini) and an ever-changing selection of seasonal dishes. The one item that never changes is the trippa alla Romana, small slices of tripe topped with a flavorsome tomato sauce, a sprinkling of mint, and plenty of Pecorino. Don't see it listed? Ask for it. If the restaurant is full, head to Passerina, the small-plates and natural-wine bar across the street, run by Giovanni's wife, Justine Passerini.

35. Pierre Sang

55, rue Oberkampf, 75011 / 6 rue Gambey, 75011

Ever since the *Top Chef* finalist and Korean-born chef Pierre Sang opened his affordable bistro on the corner of rue Oberkampf and rue Gambey, the block has been his. He expanded quickly down the road with a semi-gastronomic offering (an affordable three courses at lunch), then a bibimbap to-go shop that also houses Signature, his most formal tasting restaurant. At each place, the chef makes clear he has two great affections: French terroir—including wine, with a selection that is pulled from his personal collection—and Korean flavors, which he sprinkles into his surprise menus with great balance.

36. Le Repaire de Cartouche

8, boulevard des Filles du Calvaire or enter via 99, rue Amelot, 75011

Housemade charcuterie, a best-in-Paris pâté en croûte, plenty of game, and a deep cellar of aged natural wines have come to define chef Rodolphe Paquin's twenty-five-year-old bistro full of bon vivant regulars. But so has his legendary Sunday brunch: an all-you-can-eat buffet of rotisserie chicken, roasting in the middle of the dining room, served with creamy mushroom sauce and thick beef fat–fried potatoes; cheeses; and an array of intensely rich desserts.

37. Reyna

41, rue de Montreuil, 75011

The name of the Manila-born chef Erica Paredes's debut restaurant means "queen" in Filipino—which she absolutely is when it comes to the twice-fried chicken wings she serves with several punch-packing sauces. (Ask for the off-menu miso-honey sauce drizzled with a sesame Kewpie dressing.) Other hits include her pancit palabok, a rice noodle dish, and the vegan-friendly grilled portobello mushroom dish with adobo sauce and wild garlic pesto.

38. Le Rigmarole

10, rue du Grand Prieuré, 75011

The chef-couple Robert Compagnon and Jessica Yang have been among the city's most talented culinary disruptors since they opened this omakase-style bistro in 2017, where they introduced Parisians to binchotan-grilled dishes, fresh pastas, and homemade ice cream, served alongside a sharp natural and biodynamic wine list.

39. Le Saint Sébastien

42, rue Saint-Sébastien, 75011

Daniela Lavadenz's neo-bistro stands out for a perfect mastery of design (a Formica bar, 1950s mirrors, and forest-green banquettes), wine (natural and rare, with four hundred bottles aging in the cellar), and creative cooking that makes liberal use of seasonal vegetables and line-caught fish.

40. Septime

80, rue de Charonne, 75011

After fifteen years, countless best-of titles, and a never-ending crowd of Noma-esque culinary travelers, Septime might as well enter the Parisian Icons category. Bertrand Grébaut and Théo Pourriat's groundbreaking neo-industrial bistro experience, with its fiercely seasonal carte blanche menu, has made the rue de Charonne into the food destination it is today. Naturally, it requires a bit of luck to get a table now. Don't fret if you can't: Their excellent sister establishments, Clamato (page 103), Septime La Cave, and Tapisserie Pâtisserie, will give you the spirit of Septime and equally delicious food.

41. Le Servan

32, rue Saint-Maur, 75011

A French bistro with an Asian twist is how the French-Filipino sisters Tatiana and Katia Levha describe their much-loved neo-bistro (down the street from their second spot, Double Dragon). The ever-changing menu is dotted with dishes inspired by both their French training and their many years spent living across Southeast Asia: trout from the Pyrénées with fava beans and ponzu gelée; cockles spiced with Thai basil; terrine with black soy beans; boudin noir wontons; and a more classic Paris-Brest for dessert.

42. Le Tagine

13, rue de Crussol, 75011

It was an unorthodox pairing from the start and remains a rarity for Moroccan restaurants in Paris, but couscous, tagine, and natural wine have been the claim to fame of this 11th arrondissement restaurant since it opened more than forty years ago. Its owners, Marie-Josée and (the late) Michel Mimoun, were focused on serving low-intervention wines several decades before they would be the neighborhood's big draw. The emphasis on quality wines that respect body and earth goes hand in hand with Marie-Josée's insistence on using only the best ingredients from small producers and farmers for her menu of ten different types of couscous and a variety of tagine specials.

43. Taverna

56, rue Amelot, 75011

In a district overflowing with neo-bistros, chef Paul-Henri Bayart and his Cypriot-French wife, Margaux Varnavidou, bring Greek-Cypriot flavor to this stretch of the 11th arrondissement near the Bastille with their wine bar–meets–taverna.

The duo worked wonders with a compact two-floor space: A stainless steel and aluminum counter with bar stools flanks the ground-floor open kitchen, while a sleek communal table is the focal point of the upstairs dining room. Go for made-to-order sandwiches and salads at lunch or a flavorful series of mezze in the evening, paired with plenty of Greek natural wine.

44. La Taverne de Zhao

49, rue des Vinaigriers, 75010

This Chinese bistro near the Canal Saint-Martin was the starting place for Baoyan Zhao's restaurant group and continues to be packed with regulars from noon to night more than a decade later. Everything is a hit, from the biang biang noodles to the steamed momos (dumplings), but be sure to order the liangpi (cold noodles) and pot en terre (soup broth), which are only available at this location.

45. Le Train Bleu

1st floor, Gare de Lyon, place Louis Armand, 75012

A living museum that's awe-inspiring not only to look at but to dine in, too, Le Train Bleu is a listed landmark from 1900 inside the Gare de Lyon with 250 tables, soaring ceilings, and immense frescoes and gilding. It got a refreshed menu a few years ago when it was acquired by the grand chef and restaurateur Michel Rostang. The food is still very French—right down to the cheese trolley and the crêpes au Grand Marnier dessert prepared and flambéed at the table—but with a more elegant flair.

46. Urfa Dürüm

58, rue du Faubourg Saint-Denis, 75010

Rain or shine, this pocket-sized Kurdish sandwich shop does brisk business with its lahmacun, flatbreads topped with minced meat, onions, and tomatoes; and dürüm kefta, a rolled sandwich made with unleavened flatbread and filled with marinated grilled meat or veggies with feta (a vegan option is available, too), all gently priced. Watch the chef roll out, knead, and bake the dough at a workstation in the window while the meats cook on skewers on the charcoal barbecue grill right behind him.

47. Le Verre Volé

67, rue de Lancry, 75010

Opened in 2000, this is the earliest example of the cave à manger, known for its deep selection of low-intervention grower wines. It's easy to make an entire meal out of the small-plates menu here, which changes daily. You might see white tuna fritters with a red cabbage salad or grilled beef from the Pays Basque and mashed potatoes with piquillo peppers.

48. Waly-Fay

6, rue Godefroy Cavaignac, 75011

For more than twenty years, this industrial loft-like dining room has been churning out West African fare to a packed house. You'll find specialties from Senegal, Cameroon, and the Ivory Coast like the Thieboudienne, a one-pot rice recipe considered Senegal's national dish; chicken yassa (braised chicken with onions); mafe (peanut stew); and Cameroonian ndolé stew with mixed nuts, ndoleh (bitter leaves), and shrimp.

10th, 11th, 12th ARRONDISSEMENTS SHOPPING

These former working-class neighborhoods with industrial pasts are full of atypical spaces that once played host to craftsman workshops and artist studios and are now intriguing backdrops for home and kitchen decor shops. And as the enduring epicenter of the bistronomy movement and natural wine bar scene, they are also some of the best areas in town to shop French and European wines, local specialty food products, and artisan breads with and without gluten.

1. AXS Design

12, rue Saint-Sabin, 75011

Make a point of visiting this design-lover's treasure trove, at the back of a courtyard near Bastille, for rare decorative items, vintage tableware, linens, lighting, and even furniture unearthed from France's best brocantes (flea markets). Owners Ariel Novak and Sydney Sabatier are skilled interior and set designers, so be sure to lean on them for suggestions (and yes, they'll ship).

2. La Bague de Kenza

106, rue Saint-Maur, 75011

At this Algerian pastry shop (the city's first when it opened in 1993), you'll find heaping piles of d'ziriates, dates filled with orange blossom cream; cornes de gazelle (crescent-shaped almond cookies); baklava; and an entire section dedicated to almond-paste sweets crafted into fun fruit shapes like prickly pears and watermelon and flavored with jam. This is a shop for hardcore sweet lovers.

3. Buddy Buddy

15, rue de Marseille, 75010

No need to wonder if nut butters and specialty coffee go together; they absolutely do—and beautifully so—at this Canal-adjacent Brussels import. Spreadables aside, this spot serves vegan pastries and a slew of original drinks like the Buddy, made with espresso, peanut butter, oat milk, and cocoa, and the Rooibos Mylk Tea: a blend of peanut butter, oat milk, rooibos tea, and vanilla, served cold.

4. Chambelland

14, rue Ternaux, 75011

This is the flagship for the city's top gluten-free bakery and tea salon, created by the biologist-baker Thomas Teffri-Chambelland. He and his business partner built a mill in the south of France where they produce rice and buckwheat flour used for thick, hearty loaves of bread (the top items are the Pain aux Cinq Grains and the Pain du Village), cookies, tarts, and cakes. Take a bunch to go along with a bag of their flour for your baking needs.

5. Chambre Noire

4, boulevard Jules Ferry, 75011

Funky, radically natural wines, simple small plates, guest chefs, and stripped-down yet chic decor are features that have come to exemplify a distinctly 11th arrondissement vibe. Oliver Lomeli's growing empire of Chambre Noire wine bars and cellars can largely be credited with propelling this aesthetic.

6. Le Chocolat Alain Ducasse-Manufacture

38, 40, 42, rue de la Roquette, 75011

More than ten years ago, the legendary chef and restaurant titan Alain Ducasse expanded his empire into bean-to-bar chocolate, pralinés, and ganaches, beginning here—an impressive industrial-chic boutique and production facility set up in a converted car garage. You may catch a glimpse of the team roasting, tempering, and molding from behind a glass partition when you shop. Then head to the two adjacent boutiques to try his pure-butter biscuits and specialty sorbets and ice creams.

7. La Compagnie du Mieux Boire

75, rue Saint-Maur, 75011

One hundred percent made in France is the abiding conceit at this specialty shop and tasting room. Visit for an abundance of small-batch regional producers of whisky, gin, vodka, eaux-de-vie, apéritif spirits, and ready-to-drink cocktails and tasting workshops, organized upon request.

8. Confiture Parisienne
17, avenue Daumesnil, 75012
Scan a supermarket shelf and it's clear the French are big consumers of jam, also known as confiture. Few, however, are made within Paris. This ten-year-old specialty jam shop tucked beneath the Viaduc des Arts, the arches of an old railway viaduct, is known for its unexpected flavor combinations made on-site and sold in colorful, collectible jars. Look out for distinct combos like chestnut-pear, carrot-vanilla-passionfruit, black fig with a touch of winter spice, strawberry-cherry blossom, and a jelly of rosé Champagne Jacquart, lightly topped with white Muscat grapes, pinot noir grapes, and Madagascar vanilla.

9. Delicatessen Cave
136, rue Amelot, 75011
This lo-fi wine shop run by Mireille Langlois is an 11th arrondissement go-to for its broad selection of natural wines from both the industry's cult-favorite producers as well as more niche, emerging names. Buy a bottle to go or have her pop it open for you (for a small corkage fee) to take next door to her equally rustic bar, Delicatessen Place, set up in an old shoe repair workshop.

10. Folderol
10, rue du Grand Prieuré, 75011
Who said artisanal ice cream and wine weren't a natural match? This ice cream parlor and wine bar from Le Rigmarole's Jessica Yang and Robert Compagnon combines the two brilliantly. You'll find a lengthy menu of small-batch ice creams and sorbets that change regularly (but have included the divine banana crème crue, clementine creamsicle, cold brew, and fig hibiscus) and hundreds of natural and biodynamic wines. Don't be discouraged by a line: Most are taking their scoops to go, which means there's usually room to sit inside.

11. JJ Hings
46, rue Bichat, 75010
The Chinese-Kiwi pastry chef and ice cream artisan Julia Bell turned a wildly successful pop-up into a full-time operation with this ingredient-driven shop a stone's throw from the Canal Saint-Martin. You're guaranteed to find specialty flavors (sweet corn with smoked chile caramel, masala chai ice cream with Sicilian mango compote and honey crumble, a twist on the Lamington) and formats (scoops in a sandwich, brioche bun, or ice pop) you won't come across anywhere else.

12. Julhès
54-60, rue du Faubourg Saint-Denis, 75010
These are a series of family-owned épiceries (specialty grocers) known for their variety of goods: bread and pastry as well as prepared foods; cheeses, cured meats, condiments, and pantry staples; and a vast selection of wines and alcohols, including the whiskies, gins, rums, and vodkas produced at the Distillerie de Paris, Nicolas Julhès's own distillery and the first (and only) in Paris after a century of prohibition.

13. Landline
107, avenue Parmentier, 75011
French American entrepreneur Caroline Morrison calls her shop a contemporary twist on the general store. In reality, it's far more chic than that, with navy blue shelving, parquet floors, and a sharp selection

of durable cleaning and cookware accessories, tableware, everyday fashion essentials, and toys, all ethically produced and predominantly sourced within Europe.

14. Liquiderie Cave

9, rue des Trois Bornes, 75011

You might see a handful of folks crowded around two outdoor tables and a smattering of people around a tiny bar inside, but this artisanal bottle shop is best for picking up drinks to go. (For a full-service bar experience, head to the Liquiderie Bar—a fifteen-minute walk away.) Come for well-priced French and European craft beers, hard ciders, and natural and biodynamic wines.

15. Mamiche

32, rue du Château d'Eau, 75010

An everyday bakery and then some: Mamiche (a play on "miche," a wheel of bread) bakes all the things you'd expect—baguettes, country bread, or rolls, plus breakfast pastries—but throws in a few curveballs that have become big draws for regulars. Expect jumbo vanilla cream puffs (an absolute steal), chocolate babkas, beignets filled with seasonal creams and jams, orange blossom brioche rolls, gooey cookies, and fluffy cheesecake. Less than a five-minute walk away, Mamiche Traiteur serves more prepared foods like soups, salads, and hot sandwiches, and offers packs of fresh bagels to take home.

16. Marché d'Aligre

Place and rue d'Aligre, 75012

This is among the city's oldest and most affordable open-air food and antiques markets, open every day except Monday (the other city markets are open only twice weekly). It's in a section of the 12th arrondissement renowned since Louis XIV's reign for its carpenters and cabinetmakers, who, in the eighteenth century, were said to make the finest furniture in the world. The market and surrounding area attract Parisians for their undeniable village feel, with streets that date back to the Middle Ages. The Marché Beauvau, a listed monument, is the covered annex initially built to compete with the centrally located Les Halles (see page 26). There you'll find stalls (shown at left) for several butchers and fishmongers; Early Bird, a French-Irish-owned specialty coffee roastery; Fromagerie Hardouin Langlet; and Sur les Quais, a fine goods and condiments shop.

17. Olga

3, rue Michel Chasles, 75012

First came La Buvette, the definitive (and oft-copied) wine bar; then came Olga, Camille Fourmont's cheese, sandwich, and low-intervention wine shop a block from the Gare de Lyon. Occupying a former candy store, kitted out with all the original worn wooden cabinetry, mirrors, tiled floors, and vintage display cases, Fourmont offers a tight range of seasonal cheeses and a broad selection of wines for purchase, and sandwiches that she'll compose à la minute on fresh baguettes.

18. Taka & Vermo

61, bis rue du Faubourg Saint-Denis, 75010

Why have Brie when you could have Brie stuffed with buckwheat and candied chestnuts? Or Saint-Nectaire with sanshô pepper? Laure Takahashi and Mathieu Vermorel are the city's most inventive fromagers-affineurs, carrying more than two hundred carefully selected cheeses from animal welfare–friendly farms and small-scale productions, among which you'll find the duo's more unique creations and varieties aged in the ripening cellar beneath the boutique. Tasting and cheese-saké pairing workshops are also available.

19. Ten Belles Bread
17-19, bis rue Bréguet, 75011
Some of the best sourdough bread in the city comes from Alice Quillet, Anna Trattles, and Anselme Blayney's café-bakery near place de la Bastille. The trio, who also roast their own coffee beans for their specialty coffee bar Ten Belles, work with organic flour and grains sourced from regenerative local farms for long-fermentation breads that are shaped by hand and beloved as much by chefs and restaurant owners as by locals. Grab a loaf, a seasonal Danish or tea cake, or a sandwich (half or whole) to go with your coffee.

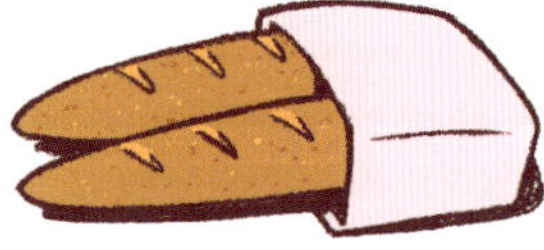

20. Utopie
20, rue Jean-Pierre Timbaud, 75011
Despite appearances, this isn't merely any old neighborhood bakery. Erwan Blanche and Sébastien Bruno regularly face lines around the block for their 100 percent sourdough croissant, sourdough breads—many featuring unexpected add-ins like muesli, matcha, or activated charcoal—and creative pâtisseries like thyme and lemon cheesecake on a sablé crust or a plum-verbena variation of the baba au rhum. If you can swing it, visit Saturday or Sunday for their more eclectic weekend bread and pastry specials.

BEYOND RESTAURANTS

Beer Bars
L'Express de Lyon
Fauve
La Fine Mousse
The Green Goose

Coffee & Tea
Café Caractère
Café Singuliers
Comets
Dreamin Man
Fauna
Kapé
Paris Dabang

Cocktail & Wine Bars
Abricot
Bambino
Bar Principal
Le Baron Rouge
La Buvette
Café Moderne
Cave Canaille
CopperBay
Dirty Lemon
Fréquence
Giclette
Martin
Minibar
Passerina
Le Syndicat

Chocolate, Pâtisserie, Bread & Ice Cream
Bake
Le Bon
Broken Biscuits
Café Mirabelle
La Chocolaterie William Artigue
Du Pain et des Idées
Frappe
La Pâtisserie Cyril Lignac
Raimo Glacier
Tapisserie
Yann Couvreur

SPOTLIGHT: DRINKING IN PARIS

Paris is a drinking city as much as it is a dining capital. In the last fifteen years, craft cocktails and beer, as well as local spirits and more radical natural wines, have risen in the ranks, rivaling the creativity and offerings of any of the world's best drinking destinations.

A made-in-France focus

Among the biggest changes to Paris's beverage scene is an enduring movement to preserve French spirits and home-grown bitters, says David Lebovitz. "France is arguably the best producer, historically, of wine and spirits," says the bestselling cookbook author of *My Paris Kitchen* and *Drinking French*. "While some older French drinkers have stopped drinking hard liquors, the younger generation has rediscovered them, celebrating them along with other made-in-France products." As such, French spirits like Cognac, Chartreuse, Pineau des Charentes, Calvados, Suze, and others are back in the limelight.

At **Le Syndicat**, a 10th arrondissement speakeasy, it's "grandpa spirits" (as the owners call them) like Armagnac, absinthe, and blanche de Normandie (apple brandy) that serve exclusively as the base for an award-winning selection of creative cocktails. **Cravan**, Franck Audoux's 16th arrondissement Art Nouveau bar, and the multistory bigger sister in Saint-Germain-des-Prés (page 77), play up original recipes that lean heavily on French wine, Champagne, and spirits. The Royals, Audoux's signatures, are cocktails that mix vintage Moët & Hennessy Champagnes (Ruinart, Veuve Clicquot, Mercier, and Dom Perignon) with subtle hints of plant-based ingredients, while his cocktails incorporate homemade cordials and infusions and highlight, as much as possible, French Cognac, gin, and other spirits (the Yellow, his standout short drink loosely based on a French recipe from the 1920s, features gin and yellow Chartreuse).

The World's 50 Best–rated cocktail bar **Little Red Door** in the Marais runs a Farm to Glass program spotlighting French fruit and vegetable producers and herb farmers. Each cocktail is built around a single ingredient from one individual producer, to honor the vendors and a more local, low-waste supply chain, says bar director Alex Francis.

Up in Belleville, Margot Lecarpentier's award-winning bar **Combat** not only uses French spirits but no-waste tinctures. "She uses leftover orange rinds and fig leaves from her parents' garden in Normandy for syrups and infusions that might be used to approximate more tropical flavors, like coconut," says Lebovitz. "It's that approach that led to the way many French spirits were invented. What does one do with all these pears or apples? Distill them and make liquor."

One example is Mathieu Sabbagh, who makes his range of Sab's Alambic Bourguignon by traveling village to village with his copper still and distilling grape marc and wine lees from Burgundy's best terroirs—a fading century-old tradition. Once bottled up, his spirits land at top bars like **Pétrelle** (page 151), **The Cambridge Public House** (page 13), **Maison Plisson** (page 22), and **La Compagnie du Mieux Boire** (page 111).

Le Syndicat
51, rue du Faubourg Saint-Denis, 75010

Cravan
165, boulevard Saint-Germain, 75006

Little Red Door
60, rue Charlot, 75003

Combat
63, rue de Belleville, 75019

An evolution in natural wine

If 2013 was a pivotal moment in the acceleration of la bistronomie as a food movement, it was equally as noteworthy for natural wine. "Parisian wine culture goes in cycles, and the past decade or so has been one of the most significant in recent memory," says Jon Bonné, the preeminent wine writer and author of *The New French Wine*. It's when the caves à manger and wine bars **Septime La Cave**, **La Buvette**, **Le Mary Celeste** (page 16), and **Chambre Noire** (page 111) opened their doors, ushering in a new wave and spirit of drinking natural wine that was big on novelty and discovery. "They were a bit underground and radical in their ways. Naturally, these spots became destinations for a sort of pilgrimage of wine and food people from the US, Scandinavia, and Japan," explains Bonné. "The momentum that would end up replicating itself in many other global cities absolutely originated in this little slice of eastern Paris."

Ten years on, many of these still-beloved, seminal wine destinations have shifted to an even more unapologetically natural wine fringe with a dominance of Italian and Spanish wines—that drinkers either love or hate. But there are plenty that take a different stance and have moved away, as Bonné puts it, from the "*tell me who you are and I'll tell you what to drink* gestalt games of the previous natty wine era" to those who "appreciate the broader world of natural wine."

Among his favorites is **Giclette**. "The owner, Guillaume Dupré, is a veteran of the Parisian natural wine scene and offers great wines on tap. You'll also find standing fridges with the entire wine inventory so clients can browse and pull a bottle at their leisure. Dupré's wife, Kaori Endo, handles the food, which is a great mash-up of French and Japanese."

Le Saint Sébastien (page 108) remains the place Bonné always tells wine friends to go drink for dinner. "In part, that's because Daniela Lavadenz is one of the great wine buyers in Paris, finding that perfect line between natural and more broadly avant-garde. Between her and her husband, Thomas Deck, the founder of the craft beer brewery Deck & Donohue, this neo-bistro is a powerhouse for drinking in Paris."

Up in Pigalle, **228 Litres** and its sibling wine shop **La Cave Pigalle** have a broad selection, including a particularly robust Champagne offering, both meant less for the staunch natural wine crowd than the wine curious. "There's never a time I visit that I don't discover something new and eye-opening."

Septime La Cave
3, rue Basfroi, 75011

La Buvette
67, rue Saint-Maur, 75011

Giclette
13, rue Keller, 75011

228 Litres & La Cave Pigalle
3, rue Victor Massé, 75009

A PERFECT TWENTY-FOUR HOURS (AND THEN SOME) IN PARIS

8:00 A.M.

One of the most special moments of the day in Paris is early morning, as the city rumbles to life and locals head to work. Start your day by taking it all in on the terrace of **Le Nemours**, a premier people-watching location and historic café across from the Comédie Française theater on the place Colette, named for the author who lived around the Palais Royal in the early twentieth century. Perfectly situated between the Louvre and the Palais Royal gardens, it is one of the very few cafés set on a public square and has the air of an Italian piazza. Go for a croissant and a simple tartine—toasted and sliced baguette with butter and jam—or a classic omelet, and (if you're not picky about coffee) a simple espresso.

Le Nemours
2, place Colette, 75001

9:30 A.M.

Now, for a quality cup of coffee, walk ten minutes to **Café Nuances**, a third-wave coffee shop set in a former crèmerie. Coffee fans should order a freddo espresso, pour-over, or one of the seasonal milk-based drinks like the rose or popcorn latté. If you lean more toward tea, try the rose matcha latté. Take your drink to go and stroll across the place Vendôme.

Café Nuances
25, rue Danielle Casanova, 75001

10:00 A.M.

Since you'll be in close proximity to the district nicknamed Little Tokyo, stroll the streets fanning off from rue Sainte-Anne and stop for a mid-morning French-Japanese snack at **Takumi Pâtisserie.** The Japanese cheesecake, as created on the island of Hokkaido, is the main draw here and made fresh daily. They're golden as they come out of the oven, fluffy, round, and crustless. But it's also worth trying their clever twists on cream puffs in yuzu, matcha, or raspberry—they use a crème au fromage (a kind of cheesy custard of cream cheese) instead of pastry cream. You should also take a Hokkaido cheese tart to go. Here, it takes on an oblong shape and comes in flavors like black sesame, yuzu, and more.

Takumi Pâtisserie
29, rue des Pyramides, 75001

10:30 A.M.

Work your way toward the river via the Tuileries gardens, cross the Pont Royal, and head through the narrow warren of streets in Saint-Germain-des-Prés, which are dotted with art galleries and antique dealers. Within thirty minutes, you'll find yourself on rue du Cherche-Midi, the historic HQ of the beloved bakery **Poilâne** (page 83), a family-owned affair since 1932. Run by the baker and entrepreneur Apollonia Poilâne, the bakery is best known for its sourdough baked by hand on the premises in the original wood-fired oven. The loaves are big on tang and have a dense crumb. The rustic apple turnover (that occasionally gets a sweet potato twist in the autumn) should catch your eye as well as the punitions—heavenly shortbread biscuits that are the perfect kind of addictive (and travel well). Get a loaf and some biscuits to go and head nearby to pick up other essentials for a picnic lunch.

Poilâne
8, rue du Cherche-Midi, 75006

12:30 P.M.

Tucked behind the oldest department store in Europe, Le Bon Marché Rive Gauche, is its more than one-hundred-year-old sister shop, **La Grande Épicerie** (page 82). The city's premier (and most premium) food emporium carries nearly 25,000 products, including specialty condiments and pantry staples, fresh foods and prepared meals, and the widest selection of wine and Bordier butter anywhere in Paris. Hit up the deli counter, cheesemonger, and bakery section to compose your own sandwich, then dig in from a bench in the Square Boucicaut down the road, named for Le Bon Marché's founder.

Alternatively, kick back a bit at **Colorova** (page 76), a five-minute walk from the store. This twelve-year-old neo-bistro run by the innovative pastry chef Guillaume Gil serves a seasonal lunch menu (and an absolute banger of a feast for weekend brunch), which might include Ajitsuke tamago (soy sauce–marinated soft-boiled eggs) with marinated and roasted bok choy, pickled jalapeños, and Thai spring onions; miso-roasted vegetables; or lamb filet with parsnips and roasted figs—all in a beautifully bright space. Request a seat in the main dining room to watch the chefs work from the semi-open kitchen.

La Grande Épicerie
38, rue de Sèvres, 75007

Colorova
47, rue de l'Abbé Grégoire, 75006

2:30 P.M.

Walk off lunch by traversing the Luxembourg Gardens. Take your time to explore (and digest): There is an abundance of impressive plant life, floral beds, more than 500 ancient varieties of pear and apple trees, and 102 statues dating back to the nineteenth century scattered throughout, all of which makes the gardens feel like an open-air museum. Once you reach the other side, keep walking another twenty minutes (or a fifteen-minute ride by bike-share) to the heart of the Latin Quarter, where the botanical Jardin des Plantes awaits. But your true destination sits just outside of the park's grounds. **La Grande Mosquée de Paris,** a century-old Moorish mosque with Andalusian gardens and patios, has always served as a place of both prayer and calm. And many come to use the hammam and sip mint tea in the tea salon, which is what you should take a break to do. Pair the tea with gazelle horns, baklava, and a variety of other North African pastries.

La Grande Mosquée de Paris
39, rue Geoffroy-Saint-Hilaire, 75005

4:30 P.M.

At this point in the day, it's been several hours since your last classic French pastry, and that must be rectified. Since there is nothing more French than a goûter—an afternoon sweet snack—it's an essential next stop. Take a twenty-minute metro on line 7 or keep the legs moving with a thirty-minute walk to reach the place des Vosges outpost of **Carette**, the Art Deco tea salon that first opened in 1927 on the place du Trocadéro. This location on the oldest planned square in Paris sits beneath its vaulted arcades with terrace seating that customers angle for even when temperatures dip below freezing. Wherever you sit, the key is to order the chocolat Carette, a velvety hot chocolate that comes with a stainless-steel coupe overflowing with a thick and fluffy cloud of whipped cream. Skip the savory menu; skip the macarons; focus on the hot chocolate and, if your appetite allows, a housemade croissant or oversized palmier whose recipe hasn't changed since the twenties.

Carette
25, place des Vosges, 75003

6:00 P.M.

It's time to leave the sweets behind and move into more serious liquid business. A ten-minute walk away is

Le Mary Celeste (page 16), which has been a pioneering anchor for natural wine, creative cocktails, and seafood-heavy small plates for more than a decade. Since you'll be ready to sip and nibble before the kitchen opens at seven P.M., your snack options will be more limited. But you can still try the one dish that never leaves the menu: les oeufs du diable, or deviled eggs. Here, they're filled with sesame mayonnaise and topped with fresh ginger, shallots, deep-fried wild rice, and spring onions. They pair well with creative cocktails and orange wines, Deck & Donohue craft beer on tap, and Lutèce, co-owner Josh Fontaine's own Parisian spirit with a gentian base that's vivacious on its own over ice or mixed with tonic.

Le Mary Celeste
1, rue Commines, 75003

7:30 P.M.

Head north, on foot or by taxi, to Belleville, where you (hopefully) booked ahead for dinner at **Cheval d'Or** (page 172), the ultimate embodiment of how exciting and globally minded dining in Paris is today. A Chinese restaurant since 1987, it was taken over by a talented quartet in 2023 who brought something fresh and new to the neighborhood. Filipino-Australian chef Hanz Gueco leads the French-Chinese menu with clever and balanced dishes that serve as flavorful reminders that "fusion" doesn't have to be a dirty word. Choose between a six-course tasting menu for the table or a nine-course carte blanche, both of which feature cold and hot starters, sizable fish and meat mains, and divine desserts. Either way, you want to ensure you've tried the fresh pasta ragu à la mapo tofu, the canard à l'orange (half or whole) with hoisin sauce, and the intriguing take on an Île Flottante (floating island) for dessert, the classic combination of a meringue cake floating in crème anglaise revisited to call to mind boba tea with tapioca pearls and caramelized almonds.

Cheval d'Or
21, rue de la Villette, 75019

9:45 P.M.

Since you're already up in Belleville, stick around the neighborhood for a first round of drinks at **Kissproof** (page 173). The Beirut-born bar has a stellar cocktail menu, organized by format and style, and an entire list of absinthes (chances are good you'll be offered a shot before the night is over). If and when you shift into wine, you have a wealth of rieslings to choose from—the owners have made it their mission to celebrate what they feel is an underrepresentation of an excellent varietal. Once the eighties to nineties revival playlist kicks into gear and the drinks keep flowing, you'll be ready for a snack before you move on for the night. The bar offers a proper dinner menu, a mix of shareable plates and comforting mains like smoked labneh and stracciatella drizzled with togarashi oil or, for something more substantial, the all-star chipotle-lime chicken sandwich.

Kissproof
50, rue de Belleville, 75020

11:30 P.M.

Paris isn't only for the drinkers and schmoozers, it's great for live music. Take a fifteen-minute cab ride to the Parc de la Villette, where, smack in the middle of the park, between the Zénith arena and the Cité des Sciences museum, **Cabaret Sauvage** has been known for its multicultural and cross-genre concerts, performances (including dance and circus), and club nights since 1997. Some advanced planning is required, though, so if you prefer to be more spontaneous, head across the park to **La Gare-Le Gore**, an atypical venue in an abandoned train station at the edge of the city. Until one A.M. there's free admission for live jazz concerts in what used to be the station's concourse. For true clubbers, it's best to stick around until later when (for a fee) the underground section of the venue transforms into a club with electronic and house music. Simple cocktails, beer, and cheap snacks are available, but you'd be better served reserving your appetite for a late-night bite elsewhere. But before you embark on your next meal, make another stop on the music circuit with a final glass at **Bambino**. This listening wine bar, open until two A.M. near the North Marais, is a draw for its shelves lined with vinyl, a stylish late-night crowd that invariably includes food industry folks as they finish their shifts, DJ sets, and cocktails on tap.

Cabaret Sauvage
59, boulevard Macdonald, 75019

La Gare-Le Gore
1, avenue Corentin Cariou, 75019

Bambino
25, rue Saint-Sébastien, 75011

2:30 A.M.

Unlike New York City or Berlin, Paris is a city that sleeps. Quality options for staying out late are limited, particularly if your goal is to eat after a long night of bar- and club-hopping, because most kitchens close by eleven P.M. What Paris lacks in diners it makes up for in a handful of legendary all-night brasseries like **Au Pied de Cochon**. Located in Les Halles and dating back to 1947, it is one of the last remaining relics from the neighborhood's eight-century run as Europe's largest food market. Depending on your cravings, you might order snails, marrow, candied pork loin, beef filet or maybe just something sweet, like profiteroles with warm chocolate sauce—until closing at five A.M. (though not for long; the doors reopen at eight A.M.). But to camp out somewhere more vibrant, with music and a hip crowd that often includes famous faces (Erykah Badu, Rihanna, and Lenny Kravitz to name a few), get yourself to **Babylone Bis**, an Afro-Caribbean restaurant in the 2nd arrondissement that stays open until six A.M. You can celebrate your marathon of a day in Paris with a round of accras, fried plantains, and braised chicken.

Au Pied de Cochon
6, rue Coquillière, 75001

Babylone Bis
34, rue Tiquetonne, 75002

7:00 A.M.

After an epically rich day of dining, the ideal cure is a sourdough croissant, a sesame roulé (a spiral-shaped pastry), and a loaf of Sencha green tea and puffed rice bread from **Utopie** (page 114). A standout in the 11th arrondissement that opens at seven A.M., this boulangerie-pâtisserie is known for its sourdough bread game and an award-winning baguette that's on par with its stellar pastry and viennoiserie offerings—and the cult following that goes with such a reputation.

Utopie
20, rue Jean-Pierre Timbaud, 75011

8:00 A.M.

A few blocks away on foot you'll find **Fauna**, an excellent specialty coffee shop opened by Jacob Köhler and Filip Josefsson, a Swedish pair of Parisian coffee industry veterans. The space is warmed by forest-green banquettes, candlelight on every table, and a comforting menu that includes housemade kanelbullar (Swedish cinnamon buns) and cardamom knots, seasonal fruit granola, and mini sourdough sandwiches filled with hard-boiled egg slices and cheese. It's all the fuel you need to continue exploring the city.

Fauna
12, rue Oberkampf, 7501

Arc de Triomphe
Champs-Élysées
Madeleine
Maison de la Radio
Trocadéro

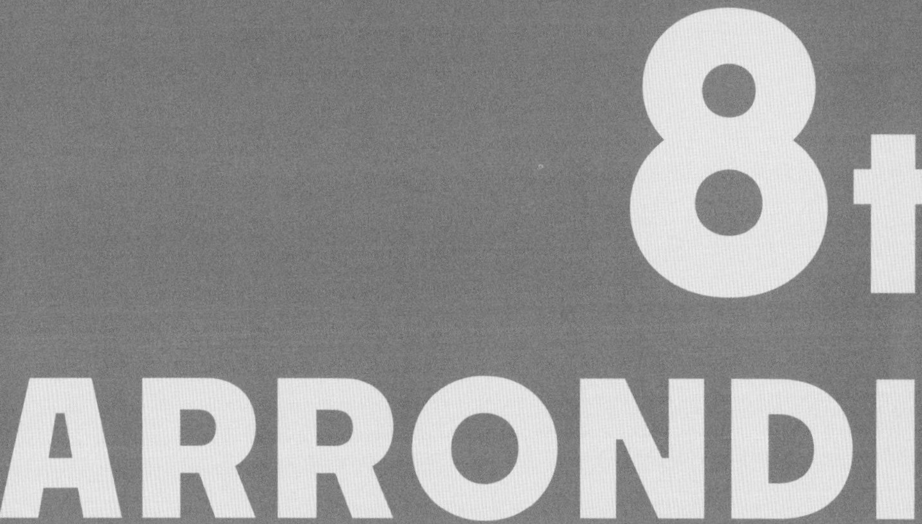

5

n, 16th

SEMENTS

AVENUE DES CHAMPS-ÉLYSÉES
PARC
MONCEAU
2
ARC DE
TRIOMPHE
17
18
16
9
1
16e
AVENUE KLÉBER
3
19
AVENUE D'IÉNA
2
6
12
AVENUE GEORGES MANDEL
TROCADÉRO
7
1
MAISON
DE LA RADIO
ET DE LA MUSIQUE
6
5
3

8th, 16th ARRONDISSEMENTS

MALESHERBES
BOULEVARD HAUSSMANN
8e
MADELEINE
RUE DU FAUBOURG SAINT-HONORÉ
ÉGLISE DE LA MADELEINE
GRAND PALAIS
PLACE DE LA CONCORDE

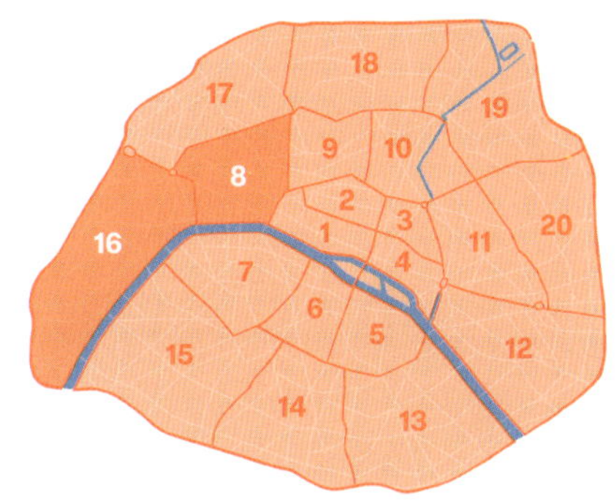

SHOPPING

1. Boissier
2. Bonnat
3. Fromagerie La Fontaine
4. La Maison du Chocolat
5. La Maison du Whisky
6. Marché Président Wilson
7. Mariage Frères

DINING

1. Le 39V
2. L'Astrance
3. Beefbar
4. Caviar Kaspia
5. Comice
6. Daroco 16
7. Ducasse sur Seine
8. Le Gabriel
9. Ladurée
10. Lucas Carton
11. Mandoobar
12. Les Marches
13. Le Mermoz
14. Néva Cuisine
15. Nonos & Comestibles
16. Pages
17. Prunier
18. Restaurant Alan Geaam
19. Substance

8th, 16th ARRONDISSEMENTS DINING

To say that Paris takes a radically ritzy turn between the place de la Madeleine and the place du Trocadéro isn't hyperbolic; it's a reality evident in the opulent real estate in these parts of the city.

Beginning from the Church of the Madeleine, around which sits a number of historic dining establishments like Lucas Carton and Caviar Kaspia, there's no mistaking the flaunty affluence of the 8th arrondissement. Dotted with high-end shops, fine art galleries, embassies, and impeccable landmarks, the district culminates with the lavish hotels and couture houses of the Golden Triangle—the epicenter of French luxury, where the Champs-Élysées, avenue Montaigne, and avenue George V, among the world's most expensive avenues, converge. Naturally, with such a concentration of high-end hotels and businesses, the restaurants tend to veer pricey. It's also why you'll find many of the splurge restaurants (more on that on page 136) in this part of town.

Cross the Arc de Triomphe via the chaotic traffic circle at place de L'Étoile and you'll find yourself in the 16th arrondissement, still affluent but quieter and, in many places, far more residential. Here, there are lush tree-lined streets, grand squares, immaculate Haussmannian apartment buildings, and notable architectural and cultural sites like the superb Palais de Chaillot. Built for the 1937 World's Fair, the site comprises two neoclassical pavilions, split by an expansive esplanade, that house four different museums and overlook the Trocadéro gardens. (Tourists know it best as the ideal spot to perch for postcard-perfect views of the Eiffel Tower.) Once a sleepy food desert, the neighborhood's culinary cred is steadily growing as chefs and restaurant groups set their sights beyond the increasingly saturated eastern districts.

1. Le 39V
39, avenue George V, 75008
Rare are the restaurants in the Golden Triangle that are decoratively compelling, reasonably priced, and worth telling friends about. Frédéric Vardon's cocoon of a contemporary French restaurant, tucked away six floors up in a Haussmannian building and overlooking Parisian rooftops, checks all the boxes and more. Its curvaceous, plush furnishings and serene color palette dreamed up by the interior architect Raphaël Navot make for the perfect backdrop for Vardon's terroir-driven seasonal menu and excellent, Burgundy-heavy wine list.

2. L'Astrance
32, rue de Longchamp, 75016
Known for having rejuvenated haute gastronomy in the 2000s and running a tiny, impossible-to-book restaurant, Pascal Barbot's pricey l'Astrance has been reborn after shutting down during the pandemic. Now with a new format and new location, the chef, who is reported to have invented the concept of the set menu, is offering à la carte options in addition to his surprise menu. At this iteration, you can expect more seafood and crustaceans, grilled and braised fish and meat, and a dedicated pastry chef running the dessert menu.

3.Beefbar
5, rue Marbeuf, 75008
There are few places left in Paris that deliver the same flashy feeling as Beefbar, one in a string of premium steakhouses from meat exporter Riccardo Giraudi. The menu is reliably carnivorous (and highlights sixty-month-aged Limousin beef) and served in a jaw-dropping jewel box of a dining room complete with restored stained-glass windows, frescoes, and a glass roof—all original Belle Époque features from the turn of the twentieth century.

4. Caviar Kaspia
17, place de la Madeleine, 75008
More clubhouse than café or restaurant, Caviar Kaspia has been a Parisian institution for the city's intelligentsia and cultural elite since 1927, when Arcady Fixon, a Russian émigré, brought Caspian Sea caviar to the French capital. Located on the place de la Madeleine since 1953, much of its original old-world glamour remains, from the aquamarine color palette and Limoges porcelain tableware to the carafes of chilled vodka and high-profile clientele—not to mention its signature baked potato topped with spoonfuls of black sturgeon roe (shown above).

5. Comice
31, avenue de Versailles, 75016
It's the trifecta of exquisite product-driven cooking by chef Noam Gedalof, expert wine pairings by sommelière Etheliya Hananova—whose selection leans heavily on small-scale artisan winemakers working on carefully cultivated vineyards—and warm, North

American-style service that makes Comice, the Canadian-born couple's neoclassical French fine-dining restaurant, such a reliably stellar address. The menu is ever-evolving, but you can bank on the best chocolate soufflé you've ever had, topped tableside with a scoop of mixed-vanilla ice cream.

6. Daroco 16

3, place Clément Ader, 75016

If you've come all the way to this residential part of town (perhaps to see the nineteenth-century replica of the Statue of Liberty, a gift from the city's American community perched on the man-made Île aux Cygnes in the Seine), swing by Daroco's brass- and marble-decked second neo-trattoria for reliably good antipasti, fresh pastas, pizzas, salads, and cocktails concocted by star mixologist Nico de Soto.

7. Ducasse sur Seine

19, Port Debilly, 75016

This meal might begin and end in the 16th arrondissement, but Ducasse sur Seine is exactly as it sounds: a Ducasse experience on the river (on an electric boat, to be precise). Most Parisian restaurant cruises rely on the view to make up for mediocre food, but here, the multicourse seasonal menu is on par with the sights.

8. Le Gabriel

42, avenue Gabriel, 75008

The Jacques Garcia–designed backdrop of Le Gabriel, located inside La Réserve hotel, is part of the appeal here but the star of the show is Jérôme Banctel's exquisite, creative cooking that blends nods to his native Brittany (dishes like marinated pigeon with buckwheat tuile) and Japanese flavors.

9. Ladurée

75, avenue des Champs-Élysées, 75008

Yes, the gilded, pastel-green Ladurée is an international chain, and the macarons are mass-produced, sold at airport kiosks and department stores. But you shouldn't go to this iconic boutique-restaurant on the Champs-Élysées for macarons. Go for lunch or teatime and experience the redesigned café and winter garden and the haute pâtisserie offerings with recipes updated or created by a World Pastry Champion, best served at the marble dessert bar, along with the fine teas you can easily pack in your suitcase.

10. Lucas Carton

9, place de la Madeleine, 75008

"Mythique" is how locals might describe Lucas Carton, one of the city's oldest restaurants (from 1839) in the shadow of the Church of the Madeleine. A temple of fine dining it may be, with pressed white tablecloths, sharply dressed servers, and all the original Art Nouveau decorative details—including boiseries by Louis Majorelle—but the kitchen has been refreshed in recent years with younger, more vibrant talent. Count on exquisitely executed and plated dishes, superb produce, and great finesse in service.

11. Mandoobar

7, rue d'Édimbourg, 75008

More than ten years after opening this quiet canteen with less than twenty seats, Kim Kwang-Loc and his sous chef are still preparing his fine Korean dumplings and tartares (shown opposite) in front of customers. Only now diners are far more knowledgeable about the fillings inside them, including kimchi and pork or bulgogi. Pair yours with Korean green tea or baekseju, a spice-fermented rice alcohol.

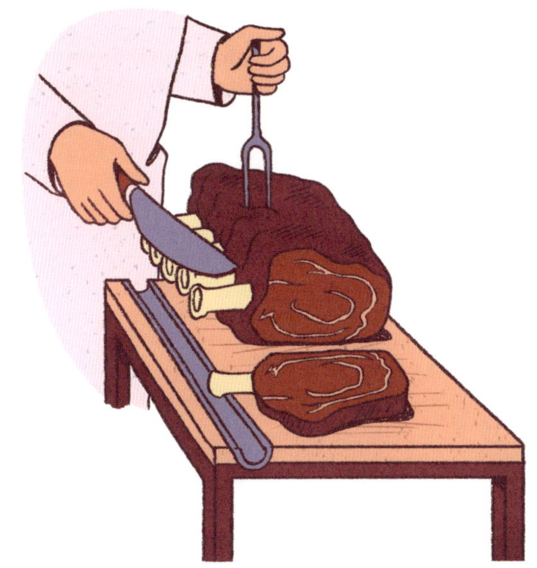

12. Les Marches

5, rue de la Manutention, 75016

One of few relais routiers (roadside restaurants) within the city limits, Les Marches goes delightfully big on nostalgia with its red-checkered tablecloths, boisterous atmosphere, and heaping portions of French classic comforts like oeufs mayonnaise and entrecôte in a thick béarnaise sauce served with perfectly crisp fries.

13. Le Mermoz

16, rue Jean Mermoz, 75008

This chef-favorite neo-bistro might seem better suited to eastern Paris, but the neighborhood is lucky to have it. A training ground for some of Paris's brightest talents, Le Mermoz always strikes the right balance between creative and traditional. Dishes may appear simple but coax out the best of each season from a who's-who of the country's finest producers. Don't skip out on excellent natural wines by the glass, which are also available at lunch.

14. Néva Cuisine

2, rue de Berne, 75008

Beatriz Gonzalez is among the most talented neo-bistro chefs in Paris, one who is well-loved by locals but little known by foreign diners. Change that by going to Néva, her first restaurant (see page 150 for her second, Coretta). You'll find bright and creative twists on classic dishes, with a particular affection for veal sweetbreads, which she cooks "croustifondant" (crispy and tender) and serves with ever-changing sides.

15. Nonos & Comestibles

6, rue Boissy d'Anglas, 75008

For his first European project after twenty years of experimental and theatrical cooking in Shanghai, Paul Pairet returned to his French roots with this 1970s steakhouse revival inside the Hôtel de Crillon. Comestibles offers all-day dining with a tight menu of cured meats and bar snacks while Nonos goes hard on cheese soufflé, grilled meats, and fish (including a standout seafood vol-au-vent)—all cut and dished up directly at each table (shown above)—and a spectacular onion soup.

16. Pages

4, rue Auguste Vacquerie, 75016

Chef-owner Ryuji Teshima is one of several exceptional examples of a Japanese chef coming to Paris to train à la Bocuse and staying to develop their own style of cooking. Since opening Pages in 2014 with his wife, Naoko Oishi, that style has looked like a colorful and creative take on top-quality terroir products from across France, occasionally prepared using Japanese cooking techniques (including barbecue).

17. Prunier

16, avenue Victor Hugo, 75016

This icon near the Arc de Triomphe remains as committed to quality seafood as it was in 1872 when it was first opened by Albert Prunier. That includes the house caviar, produced in the Aquitaine since 1921 (shown above). Award-winning chef Yannick Alléno recently refreshed the menu and its classics like the sole meunière and oysters with dill-infused almond milk, but rest assured, the landmarked Art Deco interiors remain gloriously intact.

18. Restaurant Alan Geaam

19, rue Lauriston, 75016

The self-taught Lebanese chef Alan Geaam runs a mini empire of Lebanese street food spots in the Marais. But it's here, at his tasting menu restaurant in the posh 16th arrondissement, that his talents shine most and earned his cooking—a harmonious blend of modernist French with Lebanese inflection—a Michelin star in 2018.

19. Substance

18, rue de Chaillot, 75016

The neighborhood may have a sleepy reputation, but there's nothing sleepy about Substance. The young chef Matthias Marc offers an inventive, seasonal take on contemporary French cuisine with a set menu that incorporates ingredients from his native Jura region, from cheese and sausage to wine. An equally compelling draw, however, is the Champagne list, selected with the help of Anselme Selosse, the fourth-generation producer of Jacques Selosse champagne. It's among the few places you'll find the world-renowned Jacques Selosse Initial Brut cuvée available to order.

8th, 16th
ARRONDISSEMENTS
SHOPPING

The eminently posh neighborhoods that stretch from the Church of the Madeleine all the way to the Trocadéro have an equally upscale selection of food and decor shops, as well as one of the capital's best open-air produce markets. Some have thrived here for generations, others opened outposts to capture a growing market of local and tourist shoppers. There are plenty of affordable items to go around, however, so focus your attention on chocolates, teas, cheeses, and sensational whiskies.

1. Boissier
48, rue de Passy, 75016
Since 1827, when the confectioner Bélisaire Boissier launched his namesake brand, the elegant Maison Boissier has been known for its candies, chocolates, and candied chestnuts (the glazed technique is said to have been invented by Boissier himself) in boxes and tins featuring work by top nineteenth-century illustrators—designs still used today. This makes an ideal stop for gifts and souvenirs you'll wind up wanting to keep for yourself.

2. Bonnat
189, rue du Faubourg Saint-Honoré, 75008
Whether or not Bonnat is, in fact, the oldest family-run chocolaterie in the world as it claims (circa 1884), their bean-to-bar chocolate is some of France's very best. From the original roasting site in the French Alps, Stéphane Bonnat oversees production of assorted individual chocolates, discs for baking, and milk and dark chocolate bars. If you bring only one variety home, make it the grand cru single-origin bars encased in old-fashioned, colorful wrappers.

3. Fromagerie La Fontaine
75, rue Jean de la Fontaine, 75016
It's a common story these days: A young entrepreneur takes over one of the oldest specialty shops in the city. In this case, it's a cheese shop from 1890 that was almost certainly responsible for introducing Marcel Proust, who was born on the same street, to Brie de Meaux and other fine cheeses during his childhood. Despite its small stature, the shop manages to fit a hundred different cheeses, mostly unpasteurized and some matured in-house, as well as homemade quince paste, jams, and other artisanal deli items.

4. La Maison du Chocolat
8, boulevard de la Madeleine, 75009
Since it first launched in 1977, La Maison du Chocolat has influenced the country's greatest chocolatiers. The retail locations are now spread across France and have even landed in New York. But it's Nicolas Cloiseau, a Meilleur Ouvrier de France who has overseen production and creative development since 2012, who has carried the brand into the future with innovative flavors (including savory chocolates), new formats, large artistic creations, and updates to house classics, from macarons to ganaches and other bonbons.

5. La Maison du Whisky
20, rue d'Anjou, 75008
Since 1956, La Maison du Whisky has been the leading whisky importer and distributor throughout France. At this HQ location, it stocks some 1,300 whiskies, including many rare and exclusive batches only available here, in addition to French spirits, rum, and nonalcoholic options.

6. Marché Président Wilson

Avenue du Président Wilson, 75016 (between rue Debrousse and place d'Iéna)

The stalls along the open-air Président Wilson market, the city's largest, stand at the foot of several museums—the Palais Galliera, the Musée d'Art Moderne de Paris, and the Palais de Tokyo—and stretch along the avenue du Président Wilson. Every Wednesday and Saturday, the market draws a chic 16th arrondissement crowd and discerning food shoppers who know it as a one-stop shop for sensational produce, meat, cheese, fish, and bread.

7. Mariage Frères

17, place de la Madeleine, 75008

Tea brands abound in Paris but few are as globally iconic as Mariage Frères, which opened its first tea shop in 1854. The familiar varieties are in abundant supply, but the real reason to shop here is for the hundreds of others, in various collections and collectible canisters, that you've likely never heard of before. You'll find locations across the city, but head to this one for a quiet shopping experience.

BEYOND RESTAURANTS

Coffee & Tea

Café Dior
Café Nuances
Noir

Cocktails & Wine

Le Bar du Bristol
CopperBay Lancaster
Cravan
Saint James Paris

Pâtisserie & Chocolate

Carette
L'Épicerie du Bristol
Louis Fouquet
Maison Mathieu Pacaud
La Meringaie
La Pâtisserie Cyril Lignac
Patrick Roger

SPLURGES

There are enough award-winning restaurants in spectacular settings in Paris to fill a lifetime of special occasions. Many of them come with sky-high prices, as you might expect, but if you're up for it, they're worth the splurge.

Alléno Paris
8, avenue Dutuit, 75008
The Michelin all-star Yannick Alléno goes about things differently than other upper echelon chefs. After reserving at Alléno Paris, guests receive a call from his concierge team to align on the desired parameters of their meal together. Regardless of your preferences, the meal unfolds as an exciting introduction to the chef's obsession with fermentation and techniques of extraction for creating his sauces. The experience is modern and full of the pomp and circumstance befitting a three-star in the neoclassical Pavillon Ledoyen, a building off the Champs-Élysées that has housed restaurants since 1792. Today, it's occupied not only by Alléno Paris but also by Yannick Alléno's two other starred restaurants, L'Abysse and Pavyllon.

L'Arpège
Alain Passard's three-Michelin-star ode to nature and plant-first cooking (page 75) has been going strong near the Rodin Museum since 1986.

L'Astrance
This is not only the new and improved home of Pascal Barbot, one of the city's culinary legends, but a window into the chef's unmatched prowess handling best-of French ingredients (page 129).

Le Clarence
31, avenue Franklin Delano Roosevelt, 75008
If part of what you like about fine dining is being pampered and transported, Le Clarence more than delivers. Set within a nineteenth-century private mansion done up in Grand Siècle style, the restaurant was designed to resemble the Château Haut-Brion, the legendary Bordeaux wine estate run by Prince Robert of Luxembourg, who also owns Le Clarence. Everything about the decor is grand (tapestries, paintings, opulent chandeliers, and antique furniture), which contrasts nicely with Christophe Pelé's modern land-sea menu and minimalist plating.

Le Grand Restaurant
7, rue d'Aguesseau, 75008
As boastful as it seems to suggest your restaurant is grand, Jean-François Piège's tribute to historic French regional dishes and products deserves the qualifier. Terroir-driven and largely free of fats, the experience is always playful and surprising—much like his intimate dining room that commands attention with its bold geometric skylight and Baccarat wall sconces.

Le Jules Verne

You may think dining inside the Eiffel Tower is the main draw here. While that and the view certainly add to the experience, you're coming for Frédéric Anton's modern French cooking (page 77) and his pastry chef's exceptional dessert program, which make the affair even more memorable.

Kei

5, rue Coq Héron, 75001

Kei Kobayashi is known for three things: his bleached-blond hair, his love of French gastronomy, and his namesake restaurant, done up entirely in soft gray, which earned him the honor of being the first Japanese chef in France to have his restaurant awarded three Michelin stars. His neoclassical French cooking is precise and highly technical, obvious from his signature salad featuring forty different types of edible flowers, combining bitterness, crunch, sweetness, acidity, and a hint of kick.

Marsan

4, rue d'Assas, 75006

A native of Mont-de-Marsan in the Landes region and known for her award-winning restaurant at The Connaught in London, chef Hélène Darroze spotlights the most noble of ingredients from the French southwest at her Paris flagship, Marsan. Depending on mood and budget, guests can book from three different dining environments: the elegant communal table on the ground floor; the main dining room with small, intimate tables; or the chef's table for a more interactive experience. Each follows a set menu at lunch and dinner.

Pierre Gagnaire

6, rue Balzac, 75008

The legendary modernist chef Pierre Gagnaire may have a global dining empire and an impressive collection of Michelin stars to his name, but it's at his namesake table that you'll best experience his influence on French dining, where each dish is a creative composition.

Table

3, rue de Prague, 75012

Chef Bruno Verjus is a total culinary nonconformist. The self-trained chef didn't begin cooking until he was fifty-four years old, and he opened his restaurant near the Marché d'Aligre before the neighborhood was even remotely a food destination. Ten years and two Michelin stars later, Verjus draws in diners from around the world to eat at the wave-like counter in front of the open kitchen where he talks them through each rarefied ingredient, his suppliers, and the rare wines that line his cellar.

La Tour d'Argent

A fixture of the Parisian restaurant landscape since 1592, this is the capital's most legendary table to book for a reason (page 47). Come for the view, six floors up, of the Seine and Notre Dame Cathedral, stay for the historic duck recipes and contemporary dishes created by the Meilleur Ouvrier de France chef Yannick Franques.

SPOTLIGHT: THE EVOLUTION OF PASTRY

There is no other country where baking and pastry are treated as seriously and are as rigorously protected as professions. As of the 1220s, pâtissiers in Paris were selling their confections alongside charcutiers and butchers and were formally codified by a professional guild by the fifteenth century. Bread bakers carried a stronger reputation for the better part of the trade's existence, largely due to bread's intrinsic value as a dietary necessity. Pastry was, up until the mid-1800s, a culinary art form considered the province of the elite and largely regional. Marie-Antoine Carême, France's first celebrity chef, who cooked and baked for Talleyrand, Napoleon, King George IV, and Tsar Alexander, helped nurture that impression with a collection of new desserts, like the éclair and the soufflé, which he popularized. He also made an architectural update to the ancient Greek pièce montée of wedding and high society fame (which some argue was Carême's way of asserting pastry's role as a means of "support for Napoleon's imperial ambitions"). In Carême's version, which remains a common centerpiece at weddings, the cake is a pyramid of choux pastry bound together from top to bottom with caramel.

Nurtured by the royal court, these creations became a national point of pride and eventually led to pâtisseries popping up on nearly every street corner. "Picking up a post–Sunday mass pastry became a tradition and, by extension, the art of hosting at home around it an important social symbol," wrote the journalist and author François Blanc in his book *Le Paris des Pâtisseries.* By the time the prolific innovations of the second half of the nineteenth century made their debuts—the Saint-Honoré (see page 66), the financier, petits-fours and meringue-based desserts, and the Bûche de Noël (yule log cake)—the general public was hooked.

The birth of modern pastry

The foundation for modern pastry making, however, wouldn't be established until 1957, when Gaston Lenôtre, the preeminent French pastry chef who wrote the "bible" of French desserts, opened his first Parisian boutique and ushered in a new era for the craft. Aside from working with bright fruit flavors, his biggest and most lasting contribution was lightening traditional desserts, removing as much as 20 percent of the sugar, butter, and alcohol content, which he did thanks to new refrigeration techniques. Some of his recipes, like the Autumn Leaf, a combination of meringue, mousse, and chocolate ganache, free of crème pâtissière; and the Opera cake, an almond sponge cake layered with espresso buttercream and chocolate ganache, instantly entered the canon of classics.

As influential as Carême and Lenôtre were, no one has done more to revolutionize the modern industry than **Pierre Hermé**. Now the country's most globally recognized pastry chef, with shops and cafés around the world, he first learned to make macarons as a teen apprentice at Lenôtre in the 1970s. At Fauchon, he spent eleven years overseeing the pastry operation, reinventing classic recipes and experimenting with flavors consumers hadn't seen before in desserts, like rose—commonly used, he discovered, in Bulgarian cooking. Then at Ladurée, where his mark can still be felt today, he created the Ispahan, a combination of rose, lychee, and raspberry, in a variety of formats, on top of a staggering range of macarons in novel flavors. When he broke out on his own, opening his first shop in Tokyo in 1998 and the first of many Paris outposts three years later, he brought with him those pioneering innovations and began drawing inspiration for new ones from a seasonal structure, treating limited edition thematic ranges much like fashion houses treat their ready-to-wear collections.

Lesser known to the foreign pastry audience but no less important are **Philippe Conticini** and **Christophe Michalak**, who both paved the way at their namesake bakeries for the current generation's imaginative concepts. Conticini applied cooking methods like à la minute preparation, deglazing, and seasoning with fleur de sel, a premium sea salt from the French Atlantic coast, as a way to emphasize the raw intensity of flavors in his confections and guarantee a long mouthfeel. One of his most notable riffs, which catapulted his popularity in Paris, was his take on the Paris-Brest, a wheel-shaped pastry made of hazelnut cream–filled puffs that was invented to help promote the bike race that runs, as the name suggests, from Paris to Brest, in Brittany. Conticini added liquid praline to the hazelnut cream insert, creating a molten effect that is as visually surprising as it is delicious.

Michalak, a 2005 World Pastry Champion, first earned his reputation as the head pastry chef at the Plaza Athénée hotel and initiated recipes that would trickle down into haute pâtisserie shops and everyday bakeries. He turned the millefeuille on its side to make it more elegant and easier to slice into, served the baba au rhum in an oblong shape, and adapted the Religieuse, a historic stacked choux pastry dessert with a layer of fondant that resembles a nun's collar, with salted-butter caramel, sparking a nationwide fascination with the flavor.

Pierre Hermé
Multiple locations

Philippe Conticini
Multiple locations

Christophe Michalak
Multiple locations

The "it" place for pastry: hotels

Michalak's work also prompted consumers to push for the first time through the doors of luxury hotels, where pastry chefs would rapidly gain name recognition and go on to outshine their savory peers. By 2016, no one was generating as much attention as Cédric Grolet at Le Meurice, known for his trompe l'oeil sculpted fruits and oversized Saint-Honorés. Once a put-off for the everyday Parisian who felt too intimidated to enter luxury properties like the Plaza Athénée, the Ritz Paris, Le Meurice, and the Four Seasons George V, these places became the corridors of power, with the pastry chef creating a point of entry into the upper echelons of Parisian hospitality. Maybe someone couldn't afford a sojourn at the Ritz or a three-figure meal at the Four Seasons George V, but they could most likely splurge on a Cédric Grolet pastry at Le Meurice's on-site shop or save up for a teatime extravaganza at the Shangri-La.

"It's not a hard and fast rule, but the most interesting and exciting creations in pastry are coming out of the hotels because they have limitless financial resources and access to exceptional products," explains François Blanc. "The best flans, for example, are going to be the ones served in these hotels because they can use as much quality vanilla as they like, have plenty of time, and big teams. They also initiate many of the trends that we see in pastry shops, like Maxime Frédéric's striated pains au chocolat that have popped up in bakeries like Frappe and Union shortly thereafter."

Since launching the on-site pastry shop for **Le Meurice** in 2018, Grolet has gone on to do more than make artistic pâtisserie; he's transformed the métier and helped confer an air of celebrity to the chefs themselves. Named the best pastry chef in the world by The World's 50 Best Restaurants, his star status has only continued to rise—he runs his own namesake pâtisserie and coffee shop not far from Le Meurice, travels the world leading pastry master classes for a steep fee, and doubles as a social media personality where his community has swelled to more than 20 million followers across Instagram and TikTok.

Less bling but full of talent is Maxime Frédéric, with his boy-next-door vibe, cherubic face, unironically wild hair, and a refreshingly detached relationship with social media. He first earned the respect of the culinary world when he led pastry at the Four Seasons George V, but he's unlocked a new level of acclaim as the executive pastry chef at the **Cheval Blanc Paris** and **Louis Vuitton Café**, which sits across from the hotel and overlooks the Pont Neuf. As the latest artist to work with the brand, he created several exclusive pastries, each bearing the LV iconography and displayed like pieces of art beneath glass cloches. The wait time for a seat or to buy a monogrammed chocolate bar in the shop regularly clocks between thirty minutes and one hour. (Frédéric and his team also oversee all of the bread, viennoiserie, and pâtisserie at the Cheval Blanc's restaurants and room service menu.) And at the end of 2024, he opened PleinCoeur in the 17th arrondissement—his first family-run shop with his wife and sister.

Both the Ritz Paris and the Hôtel de Crillon on the place de la Concorde have prioritized their pastry programs, running some of the most-reserved teatimes in the city and opening to-go boutiques of their own to tap into what might aptly be called pastry tourism. **Le Comptoir**, accessible from rue Cambon, is a fast-casual boutique done up in peachy tones, leather banquettes for nibbling on-site, and hand-blown crystal light fixtures meant to mirror the bulbous side of chef François Perret's signature madeleines. A long counter elegantly displays his renditions of classic pastries, including his signature glazed madeleines, and his to-go-friendly "cake shakes"—drinkable versions of his three best-selling pastries from the Salon Proust teatime menu. At **Butterfly Pâtisserie**, the Hôtel de Crillon's jewel box of a shop, pastry chef Matthieu Carlin's elegant range of seasonal tarts, millefeuilles, breakfast pastries, madeleines, and mini cookies are presented on marble (naturally) and priced reasonably, even when indulging on-site in the adjacent boudoir-like salon.

La Pâtisserie du Meurice par Cédric Grolet
6, rue de Castiglione, 75001

Cheval Blanc Paris
8, quai du Louvre, 75001

Maxime Frédéric at Louis Vuitton
2, rue du Pont Neuf, 75001

Ritz Paris Le Comptoir
38, rue Cambon, 75001

Butterfly Pâtisserie
6, rue Boissy d'Anglas, 75008

The new guard: fruit, foreign talent, and international flavors

Of course, the innovations in pastry aren't limited to the city's most rarefied spaces. Some of the most enduring and impressive work, even when made with more modest means, has come from chefs and bakers who bring something different to the table. They combine fruit and vegetables, use Levantine spices and herbs, and jump at the chance to incorporate Asian citrus fruits, matcha, azuki, and miso. Claire Damon's **Des Gâteaux et du Pain** earns high marks for an ethical focus on using fruit at the peak of its ripeness from small-batch French producers as well as almonds grown in Provence. In refusing all additives and colorants, hers may not be the most decoratively flashy of pastries, but they are balanced and naturally sweet and address consumers' growing concerns around sourcing and sustainability.

Myriam Sabet has completely flipped Levantine pastry on its head with more refined and original recipes at the two outposts of her **Maison Aleph** (page 21). Anchored in French technique but resolutely modern, she has introduced Parisians to nids, kadaïf angel hair nests made with clarified butter and filled with flavored creams or candied fruit, and her take on the 1001 Feuilles, where layers of phyllo dough are filled with a nut mixture akin to baklava that includes hazelnuts, pistachios, sesame, and halvah. Her fruit-based tarts rotate seasonally while two luscious Bundt cakes—one flavored with pistachio and orange blossom, the other a combination of spices—are year-round classics.

Elsewhere in Paris, there's creative shortbread tarts of various sizes at **Bontemps Pâtisserie**, sesame éclairs and fruit-filled entremets (small layered pastries typically incorporating mousse) at **Utopie** (page 114), seasonal tartelettes and a pecan cake with vanilla-caramel ganache called the Isatis at **Yann Couvreur** that regularly sells out, and a hojicha (green tea) twist on the Saint-Honoré at **Pâtisserie Rayonnance** (page 155).

With an ever-expanding scene, there are hundreds of other options to satiate a sweet tooth in Paris, from bubble tea and chiffon cake to gourmet doughnuts and ice-cream-based desserts.

Des Gâteaux et du Pain
Multiple locations

Bontemps Pâtisserie
57, rue de Bretagne, 75003

Yann Couvreur
Multiple locations

Batignolles
Goutte d'Or
Montmartre
South Pigalle

9th, 17
ARRONDI

6

th, 18th

SEMENTS

9th, 17th, 18th ARRONDISSEMENTS

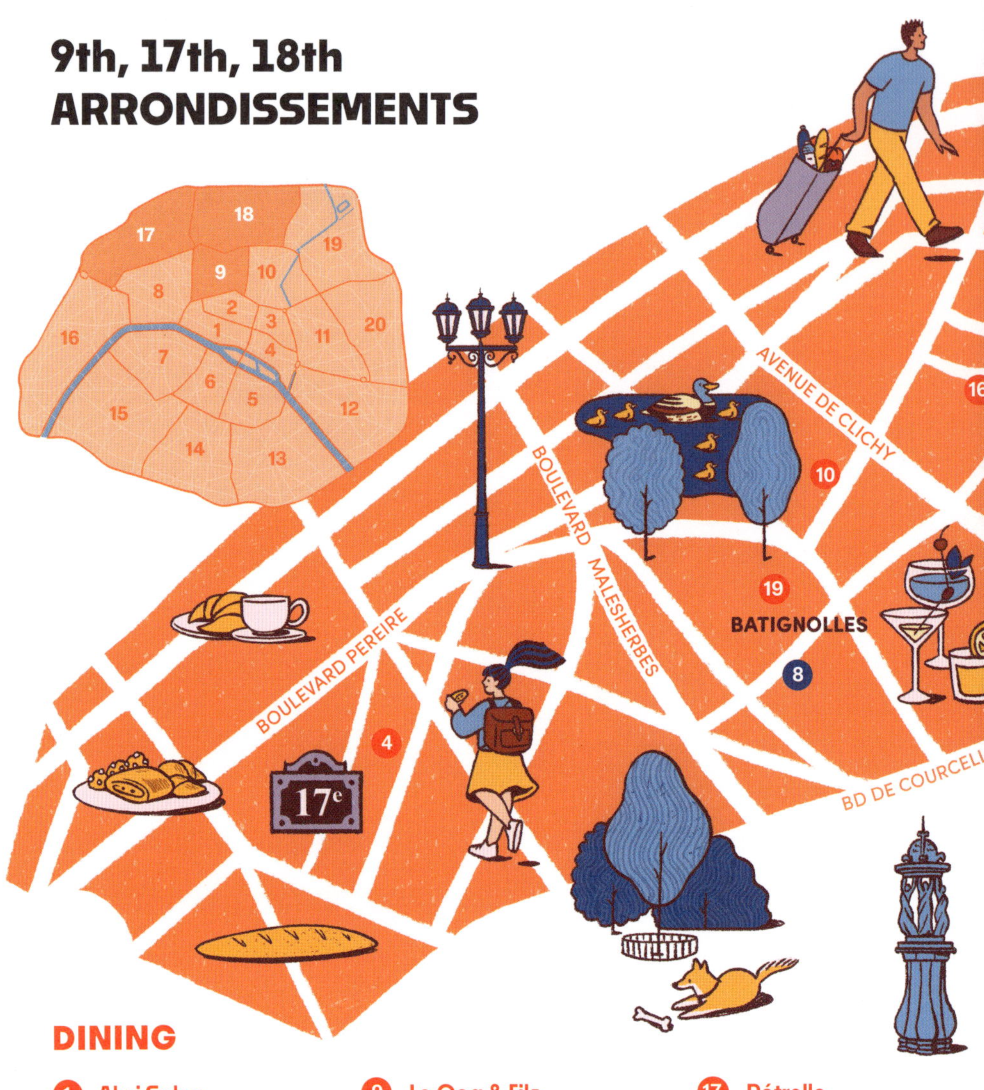

DINING

1. Abri Soba
2. a.léa
3. Au Rêve
4. Le Bistrot Flaubert
5. La Boule Rouge
6. B.O.U.L.O.M
7. Il Brigante
8. Coloré
9. Le Coq & Fils
10. Coretta
11. Cuisine
12. Le Cyrano
13. Double
14. Le Maquis
15. Mehmet
16. Mi Kwabo
17. Pétrelle
18. La Recyclerie
19. Rooster
20. Signature Montmartre
21. Le Supercoin
22. Sushi Shunei

SHOPPING

1. À la Mère de Famille
2. Atelier P1
3. Babka Zana
4. Galeries Lafayette Gourmet
5. La Laiterie de Paris
6. Lemon Story
7. Little Africa Village
8. La Maison du Mochi
9. Monbleu
10. Pâtisserie Rayonnance
11. Shinya Pain Montmartre

9th, 17th, 18th ARRONDISSEMENTS DINING

These northern neighborhoods, spread throughout the 9th, 17th, and 18th arrondissements, are some of the city's most dynamic, fun, and family-friendly. They're also spacious, with countless hidden gardens that veer off cobblestone courtyards and larger green spaces like Parc Monceau where runners, picnickers, and stroller-pushers convene daily.

Begin in South Pigalle, whose main artery is rue des Martyrs—named as such because it's where martyr Denis is said to have walked holding his own head en route to the Basilica of Saint-Denis (due north of the city), which now memorializes him and all of France's former kings and queens. Fast-forward to the mid-1800s, when this area was considered Paris's red-light district, with many bustling nightclubs and cabarets angling for the attention (and francs) of aristocrats with secrets and spare change. Things are a bit different on the thoroughfare today, as it's full of artisanal food stores, coffee shops, and kids licking ice cream cones while riding the carousel at the top.

With gentrification, South Pigalle is now decidedly less debaucherous. It's still a hub for nightlife and socializing, thanks to some of the city's most creative cocktail bars and clubs, which are often hidden behind nondescript doors or down narrow alleyways that provide mystery and allure.

Crossing the boulevard and heading farther up the hill—or the butte, as it's known—we enter Montmartre, where a variety of writers, musicians, dancers, and artists found fame at the end of the nineteenth century and well into the twentieth. The semi-stuck-in-time Moulin Rouge continues to anchor the area on boulevard de Clichy, with its bright lights signaling a show that's literally still kicking. Amid the area's landmarks (like the very underrated Musée de Montmartre) are a mix of stalwart bistros serving hearty fare and newer restaurants catering to today's discerning diners.

While aimlessly wandering the winding streets (and many staircases) can make for a lovely afternoon, the astounding views of the city as seen from Paris's popular basilica Sacré Coeur—consecrated fairly recently, in 1919—means this area is often packed with tourists. Farther west, between metro stations Villiers and Rome, however, the villagey neighborhood known as Batignolles has become what many say Montmartre once was: a place for the locals.

1. Abri Soba

10, rue Saulnier, 75009

Parisians are still mourning the shuttering of chef Katsuaki Okiyama's mind-blowing neo-bistro Abri, but it's possible to get a taste of his handiwork at Abri Soba, an izakaya where the best seats are at the counter in front of the open kitchen. There, chefs make buckwheat soba noodles from scratch for hot or cold soups, served plain, garnished with meat, or with a side of tempura.

2. a.léa

39, rue Lamarck, 75018

Montmartre insiders know that this contemporary bistro up on la butte has one of the best lunch deals in town: three seasonal, flavorful, and beautifully plated courses at an affordable price. More expensive meats and fish, like canard de Challans and sea bream, appear in more involved dishes at night. But you'll be in excellent hands for a leisurely lunch.

3. Au Rêve

89, rue Caulaincourt, 75018

A Montmartre locals' watering hole par excellence since 1921 and recognizable with its neon-blue sign, Au Rêve was saved from extinction by architects Clémentine Larroumet and Antoine Ricardou in 2023. They updated only what needed refreshing, preserving the simple charm of the rotating daily menu (maybe a risotto, or celery remoulade, or steak tartare). Or go for a croissant and "un petit noir" (espresso) and sit on the terrace, watching as the neighborhood jolts awake.

4. Le Bistrot Flaubert

10, rue Gustave Flaubert, 75017

In a seductive space that smacks of bygone Paris—marble tabletops, tall wooden shelves displaying exceptional bottles of wine and thick stacks of Michelin guides, and stained glass—the restaurateur Stéphane Manigold draws on the past with Bistrot Flaubert but disrupts with eminently creative, meticulously executed applications. Meat and fish are expertly prepared, but this is also a good spot to go vegetarian.

5. La Boule Rouge

1, rue de la Boule Rouge, 75009

Where did François Hollande spend his last meal as French president with his cabinet? At Raymond Haddad's La Boule Rouge, a Jewish-Tunisian standby in the 9th arrondissement. Lamb couscous aside, regulars know to come for the mixed kémias, loubia (a white bean stew), pkaila couscous (with spinach and beef), and spiced meatballs. Expect a special menu for Friday night Shabbat dinner.

6. B.O.U.L.O.M

181, rue Ordener, 75018

All-you-can-eat, a concept associated with the American buffet, is generally absent from Parisian dining culture (except when it comes to endlessly replenished plates of fries at certain generous bistros). But chef Julien Duboué, who hails from the French southwest, took a risk that paid off with his bakery-meets-buffet in the 18th arrondissement. The spread includes hot and cold dishes, ranging from whelks with mayo, black pudding terrine, veggie salads, beef ribs, Basque-style chicken, and an over-the-top profiteroles bar—only one of several indulgent options for dessert.

7. Il Brigante

14, rue du Ruisseau, 75018

This pocket-sized Calabrian pizza restaurant in northern Montmartre has been an insider favorite since 2012. For his thin-crust pies, chef Salvatore Rotiroti relies on the best Italian ingredients, including flour he imports from Puglia for dough that matures for thirty-six to forty-eight hours. The decor is sparse but the pizzas, as Rotiroti puts it, are maximalist.

8. Coloré

20, rue du Ruisseau, 75018

While it's tempting to reduce Coloré, chef Megumi Takehana's café in Montmartre, to a coffee shop, there's a lot more going on here that deserves your attention. Veggie udon and bright, produce-rich salads sit alongside sashimi-topped rice bowls, open-faced sandwiches on homemade milk bread, and small tapas like slow-roasted dashi leeks in the evening. Don't leave without something sweet (and seasonal), like the vegan rhubarb, orange, and coconut cake; a satsuma mandarin Mont Blanc; or one of several types of cookies.

9. Le Coq & Fils

98, rue Lepic, 75018

How good could a roasted chicken be? Life-changing, if ordered at chef Antoine Westermann's Montmartre restaurant Le Coq & Fils, known for its rotisserie birds—for one or to share—and a panoply of poultry products. The menu offers it all, from giblets and terrine to coq au vin, roasted cou nu (a French heritage breed of chicken), braised quail, and a selection titled "egg'z" for deviled eggs and other variations. You may be tempted by the fries, but the macaroni gratin is the house favorite, followed by the chef's signature egg-based Île Flottante for dessert.

10. Coretta

151, bis rue Cardinet, 75017

With its glass facade, contemporary dining room, and creative plates, chef Beatriz Gonzalez has made Coretta—named for its proximity to the Martin Luther King Junior Park—a Batignolles staple. Like most neo-bistros, the à la carte menu constantly evolves, but expect a diversity of flavors that span the globe on a foundation of stellar French products.

11. Cuisine

50, rue Condorcet, 75009

With an air of 1970s Milanese design and a name that's both comically obvious and terrible for search engines, Cuisine has nailed the izakaya-style small plates format in South Pigalle, where ingredients are sourced exclusively from organic or sustainable agriculture. A mix of French and Japanese dishes served à la carte, like karaage-style pigeon; siu mai (dumplings) with pork, shrimp, and sea urchin; and octopus salad with leeks, celery, umeboshi, wakame, and wasabi get passed among friends for dinner with endless glasses of organic and natural wines from artisan producers.

12. Le Cyrano

3, rue Biot, 75017

A quick walk from place de Clichy, this intimate bistro from 1914 was revived by four friends who kept all of the relic details intact: mosaics, marbled zinc bar, large Art Deco mirrors, and paintings under glass in homage to Edmond Rostand's *Cyrano de Bergerac*. The interior is reason enough to visit; however, the lightly modern, French menu is why you should book. Dishes like chipotle beef bourguignon with candied sweet potato, flame-cooked mackerel atop a parsnip purée, or terrine à la za'atar with pickles are served at the table or counter (for a few euros less) at lunch, while a tapas menu takes over at night and on weekends, featuring a divine potato millefeuille.

13. Double

87, rue Lamarck, 75018

Double transforms from an onigiri to-go window at lunch to a micro-restaurant with only twenty-three counter seats at dinner, serving fresh pastas. That's the concept of this fun, if unusual, Montmartre hotspot led by Japanese chef Tsuyoshi Yamakawa, who combines influences from his homeland with his passion for Italian cooking from an open kitchen. With no more than ten dishes, everything is worth trying, but his savory maritozzi, brioche buns filled here with fresh ricotta and topped with ikura (salmon caviar), are a must.

14. Le Maquis

53, rue de Cloÿs, 75018

Up on a quiet Montmartre street, this casual neighborhood bistro in a former bar was opened by a pair of Iñaki Aizpitarte disciples who cook the same ingredient-focused dishes diners love at Le Châteaubriand, but with gentler prices and far more radical natural wines. The chalkboard menu is ever-changing but covers some French classics (veal blanquette) and more borderless recipes (cockles in a spicy Sichuan broth or kimchi dumplings)—and it works every time.

15. Mehmet

43, rue Ramey, 75018

Natural wine, döner kebabs, and mezze? It all goes well together at Mehmet, a Turkish-style corner bar set behind the Sacré Coeur (it earned the Action Bronson seal of approval). Spit-roasted chicken from a small producer in Normandy is an obvious draw, along with double-fried fries and chile mayo for dipping, but don't sleep on the regional mezze like sorrel leaf–wrapped sardines with pickled onions, kisir, crispy labneh, and spicy chicken wings.

16. Mi Kwabo

44, rue Guy Môquet, 75017

At his 17th arrondissement Afro-Caribbean bistro, the self-taught chef Elis Bond takes his cooking far beyond familiar classics like mafe (peanut stew) and yassa (a spicy Senegalese dish prepared with onion and marinated poultry, fish, or lamb) to explore the broad influences, spices, and ingredients of the ever-changing cuisine. That might include fish accras (fritters) with black mayo made of mbongo, a heady blend of Cameroonian spices, or smoked and confit onion with a Senegalese soumbara béarnaise and a smoked lemon condiment, all served up on beautiful ceramic dishware.

17. Pétrelle

34, rue Pétrelle, 75009

There are countless restaurants in Paris that are ideal for date night, but Pétrelle tops the list with its antique chandeliers, abundance of dried flowers, frescoes, fringed lampshades, and most importantly, candlelit tables for two and four. Somehow even the dishes, served over four courses at dinner, read romantic in such a setting—cockle gnocchi with fresh summer tomato; green asparagus ceviche with strawberries and bee pollen ice cream; and a rhubarb millefeuille served with a scoop of tahini ice cream topped with pistachios and za'atar. Peruse the leather-bound wine list and raise a toast with one of several grower Champagnes that won't break the bank.

18. La Recyclerie
83, boulevard Ornano, 75018
This semi-hidden, multipurpose space features a café-bar, urban farm, and upcycling center and is most popular for its curious locale: La Recyclerie sits in an abandoned train station above a set of tracks on La Petite Ceinture (little belt), a defunct rail line that circles the city. Open to the public Friday through Sunday, you'll find locals strolling, sipping craft beer, or snacking from a locavore and half-vegetarian menu in a bric-a-brac space.

19. Rooster
137, rue Cardinet, 75017
After making waves at Racines in New York, the Marseille-born chef Frédéric Duca landed in Paris, where he spotlights the breadth of Mediterranean cuisine at Rooster, his upscale bistro in Batignolles. At both lunch and dinner, the menu is concise—only a few starters, mains, and desserts—but a beautiful sampling of top French ingredients with a flavorful mash-up of the cities the chef has cooked in over the years and his favorite ingredients, like mackerel, lamb, anchovy, and sea urchin.

20. Signature Montmartre
12, rue des Trois Frères, 75018
In a dense tourist pocket of Montmartre, chefs Youngrim Kim and Sungmi Lee's Signature Montmartre is a refreshing escape. In their intimate neo-bistro, the chefs were some of the earliest to nail the French-Korean crossover menu, with choices like Korean buckwheat noodles with salmon roe and red onions, vol-au-vent with wild sesame king trumpet mushrooms and black truffle, and an apple millefeuille with caramelized puff pastry, green apple compote, and a mousse of makgeolli, a fermented rice alcohol. Start the meal off with a Korean Kir Royale, which swaps the crème de cassis for omija, a magnolia berry tea, and the rest flows from there.

21. Le Supercoin
17, rue Boinod, 75018
This Montmartre neighborhood bar has all the trappings of the kind of hangout where you'd want to be a regular: excellent French craft beer and natural wine, and an affordable but thoughtful and delicious snack menu featuring sandwiches (shown above)—always a beef, sausage, and veggie option—soups, and homemade desserts of the day. Wash it all down with some of the hyperlocal beers on tap from Outland, Les Bières de Belleville, and La Brasserie du Grand Paris.

22. Sushi Shunei
3, rue Audran, 75018
"Why isn't there more good sushi in Paris?" It's a common question, but the issue isn't a lack of good sushi, but rather that it comes at a hefty price. Sushi Shunei is no different, but it's worth booking if you're curious to try this sleek, all-wood edomae sushi counter that seats nine, founded by master Shunei Kimura and now run by his widow Chizuko Kimura and chef Takeshi Morooka. You'll have a choice between two different nigiri tasting menus, both of which close with the perfect hazelnut-hojicha sorbet from the Alain Ducasse-Manufacture.

9th, 17th, 18th ARRONDISSEMENTS
SHOPPING

Some semblance of village life is alive and well in these north and northwestern arrondissements, spanning South Pigalle to Batignolles. It isn't uncommon to see locals carting their shopping bags up and down the rue des Martyrs and the rue Lepic, going from one specialty store to another for their daily provisions. Take a page from the locals and do the same: hop between historic chocolate shops and small-scale bakeries, with visits to a few concept stores in between.

1. À la Mère de Famille
35, rue du Faubourg Montmartre, 75009
A chocolate and candy empire from 1761 (among the oldest in Paris), À la Mère de Famille's wide range of bean-to-bar chocolate bars, bonbons, pops, truffles, candied fruit, coated marshmallows, and ice creams are available at shops across the city. But this historic flagship is the one to visit. Take in the nineteenth-century decor—wood paneling, antique windows, and glass display cases—and feel frozen in time.

2. Atelier P1
157, rue Marcadet, 75018
This modernist corner bakery in Montmartre is more than an excellent source for sourdough breads, organic fruit and vegetable tarts, viennoiseries, and sandwiches—it's also a place to learn bread making. P1 hosts three-hour workshops (in French only) each Wednesday, where aspiring bakers can learn the essential steps to making sourdough at home.

3. Babka Zana
65, rue Condorcet, 75009
At this Levantine bakery, you can watch the team of bakers knead, shape, garnish, spread, roll, braid, and bake their flagship product, babka, and also produce rugelach, challahs, borekas,

sweet rolls, sticky buns, and labneh cheesecake. While it's tempting to bring home one of everything sweet, don't overlook the sandwiches (roasted vegetables or smoked chicken salad) served on their homemade challah. They also run a sit-down café located a stone's throw from the place des Vosges at 8, rue du Pas de la Mule, 75003.

4. Galeries Lafayette Gourmet

35, boulevard Haussmann, 75009

Behind the Opéra Garnier, this specialty annex of Galeries Lafayette, the turn-of-the-century department store across the street, is a food lover's playground. Spanning three floors, there's a food court with casual dining spots from chefs Pierre Sang, Mory Sacko, and Thibaut Spiwack and a slew of options when it comes to sweets: the historic pâtisserie Dalloyau, Yann Couveur, Pierre Marcolini, Pierre Hermé, and Alain Ducasse all operate stands on the ground level.

5. La Laiterie de Paris

74, rue des Poissonniers, 75018

This spot in the Goutte d'Or neighborhood is more an urban cheese dairy than a shop. Each week, Pierre Coulon and his team receive fresh cow, goat, and sheep's milk, which they transform into fresh yogurts and cheeses, from Reblochon and cider-washed Camembert to labneh and burrata.

6. Lemon Story

1, rue Garreau, 75018

Bring home a taste of the south of France with a stop at Lemon Story, a small shop near Abbesses specializing in all things citrus: artisanal jams, marmalades, limoncello, and makrut lime salt. The "story" the shop's name references is a personal one for owner Marion Laperche—all the rare fruits (yuzu, Tahiti lime, caviar lemon, Buddha's hand) are handpicked and grown on her family's four-hundred-tree citrus grove in the Var (South of France). Pick up a few jars knowing that they have a chef's seal of approval—they've popped up in the kitchens at some of the city's best restaurants.

7. Little Africa Village

6, bis rue des Gardes, 75018

An anchor in the Goutte d'Or neighborhood, Jacqueline Ngo Mpii's cultural center, art gallery, and boutique is a treasure trove of goods from the Afro-Caribbean diaspora. Shop brass and gold-plated jewelry, ebony candelabras from Benin, woven placemats and bronze napkin holders from Ghana, as well as paper goods designed by Ngo Mpii and specialty food items like Madagascan chocolate, spices, and bissap juice. And if fashion is more your thing, Little Africa Village also carries a selection of handwoven two-tone raffia handbags from AAKS, an ethical brand that produces pieces with a women's collective in northern Ghana.

8. La Maison du Mochi

30, rue Legendre, 75017

Make a stop for something sweet (and something less common in Paris) at this elegant boutique specializing in daifuku (sweet, chewy, and dumpling-like with a red bean paste filling). It was during her time living in Japan that the shop's founder, Mathilda Motte, fell for mochi and its many sweet manifestations. At La Maison du Mochi, it's all about the handmade, tender daifuku in seasonal, French-Japanese flavors like almond–orange blossom, chestnut cream, yuzu, and black sesame. Pick up a box, along with a jar of chocolate praliné soba spread you'll end up eating by the spoonful.

9. Monbleu

37, rue du Faubourg Montmartre, 75009

Monbleu is a cheese shop in the front and cheese restaurant at the back. The full-fromage concept has worked wonders here, as locals visit to replenish their fridges with more than one

hundred types of cheeses, a selection curated with a Meilleur Ouvrier de France cheesemonger, and stay for wine, cheese platters, and hot cheese-based dishes like baked mont d'or, a mini tartiflette, and blue cheese, pear, and walnut gnocchi.

10. Pâtisserie Rayonnance

17, rue de Maubeuge, 75009

Yuki Hayato and Lumi Hachiya met working in fine dining—Yuki on pastry, Lumi on service—and sold made-to-order caramels, cookies, and cakes for the restaurant's clients during the pandemic lockdown. Once it took off, they knew they had the makings of a new business and launched Pâtisserie Rayonnance in 2022. At their 9th arrondissement shop, the women make romias cookies with matcha or orange blossom and almond, tigré cakes with fruit or chocolate, and individual cakes that riff on classics, like the Mont Blanc with yuzu, the Saint-Honoré with hojicha (green tea), and cheesecake using eighteen-month-aged Comté cheese.

11. Shinya Pain Montmartre

41, rue des Trois Frères, 75018

While it operates as a bakery, this compact shop at the foot of Sacré Coeur is more like a laboratory for sourdough legend Shinya Inagaki's baking experiments. You won't find baguettes here, but there is a selection of "peasant breads" made from natural sourdough and ancient grains, as well as sourdough cookies and cakes. The haphazard display is part of the charm: Inagaki lays out the loaves on baking racks and labels them by hand on Post-it notes, which he shares on Instagram daily. The windows of opportunity to try them, however, are limited: the shop is only open between Thursday and Sunday, 4:30 P.M. to 7:30 P.M.

BEYOND RESTAURANTS

Coffee & Tea

Les 5 Marches
Blondie
Café Lomi
Café Tabac
Clove Coffee Shop
Ibrik Café
KB Coffee Roasters
La Main Noire
Noir
Ola's Café
Two Doors

Cocktail & Wine Bars

Au Petit Rozey
BBP Pigalle
Billili
Classique
Dirty Dick
Lolo Cave à Manger
Mikkeller
Patoche Microbrewery
Pigalle Country Club
Poney Club
Sister Midnight
Soif
Stéréo
Le Très Particulier

Pâtisserie, Bread & Ice Cream

Bob's Bake Shop
The French Bastards
Glazed
Le Jardin Sucré
Jean-Paul Hévin
Jeffrey Cagnes
Mamiche
La Meringaie
PleinCoeur

SPOTLIGHT: SUB-SAHARAN AFRICAN AND CARIBBEAN CUISINE

Specialty stores, restaurants, and bars with Caribbean flair are scattered across Paris, in homage to the flavors and traditions of French overseas territories like Martinique and Guadeloupe. But the richness of sub-Saharan culinary heritage hasn't always been so evident. According to Jacqueline Ngo Mpii, the founder of the cultural agency Little Africa and the gallery-concept store Little Africa Village in the Goutte d'Or neighborhood, the growing prominence of this cuisine is a much more recent development—despite migratory waves dating back to the 1960s and 1970s when the population settled around Château Rouge, Château d'Eau, and more generally across the 18th arrondissement. A few of her insights:

"La Goutte d'Or has always been a place where you could find maquis—super informal, open-air restaurants from the Côte d'Ivoire where you sit down and eat shoulder to shoulder with others, but you don't expect traditional service or even a menu, necessarily. It's these kinds of spaces that kicked off African cuisine in France as a way to connect people from within a similar community and create a link to the country or countries left behind. As I was growing up, nobody was talking about West African cooking, so we had to experience that cuisine in more personal spaces like ceremonies or parties but rarely at any formal restaurant. It felt, for a long time, that we did not exist. What we're seeing today only started about fifteen years ago. It began with high-end restaurants in the 16th arrondissement where many of the African ambassadors and diplomats lived, but those spots didn't last long. Then came chefs like Dieuveil Malonga and Loïc Dablé who brought a very contemporary view of African cuisine. They understood that an emphasis on plating, aesthetics, and blending Western tastes with African ingredients would be a way to give the cuisine its own place in Paris. That's when people started talking about Afro-fusion, an approach that still exists very much to this day.

"You can see it—and taste it—in action at **Waly-Fay** (page 109), which has adapted specialties from Senegal, Cameroon, and the Ivory Coast for the last twenty years, at **New Soul Food-Le Maquis**, known for its mix of soul food and Afropean cooking, at **BMK Folie-Bamako** (page 102), with its two Malian restaurants in the 10th and 11th arrondissements. Beyond that, you'll also find a smattering of restaurants that are vegan, which reflects the way many families, including my own, eat in West and Central Africa given that animal proteins, such as chicken or beef, are expensive, urban staples. Places like **Jah Jah** (page 105) and **L'Embuscade** highlight this cooking perfectly."

Today, chefs and restaurateurs descended from Afro-diaspora cultures serve up dishes that speak to the Parisian palate. The most marked change has been brought about by dynamic young chefs, including Mory Sacko, whose restaurant **MoSuke** (page 46) earned a Michelin star after a year of opening in 2020. Sacko, who graced the cover of *Time* magazine in 2023, has cooked for President Macron at a summit on Africa. At MoSuke, he is known for mixing West African staples with his passion for Japanese culture—he's a hardcore manga fan—and his rigorous fine-dining training. The result: the beef for his signature beef mafe stew is matured in shea butter before being grilled on a Japanese barbecue and served with peanut sauce. The stew also weaves in katsuobushi, or fermented tuna. His chocolate dessert is infused with wasabi; and the sashimi is made not with rice but West African attiéké, or cassava semolina.

And at **Mi Kwabo** (page 151), the French-Haitian-Guyanese chef Elis Bond harnesses French cooking techniques with local fruits and vegetables from the Vergers Saint-Eustache, and African products and spices from the Château Rouge neighborhood. At the end of each service, he goes table to table showing guests the raw ingredients he used to prepare each dish.

New Soul Food-Le Maquis
177, quai de Valmy, 75010

L'Embuscade
47, rue Catherine de la Rochefoucauld, 75009

THREE PARISIAN-APPROVED OVERNIGHT TRIPS

If you're sticking around Paris for more than a few days, consider a weekend trip to Champagne, Brittany, or Provence, parts of France beloved by locals and full of great dining, drinking, shopping, and outdoor activities.

TRIP 1: Champagne

by Julia Coney

Julia Coney has built her entire career around wine. The journalist, consultant, and educator, based between Houston and Washington D.C., has been the wine consultant for American Airlines in partnership with the James Beard Foundation; pioneered Black Wine Professionals, a resource for wine industry employers and the food and beverage community at large; and has been active in pushing for greater diversity, inclusivity, and equity in the wine industry—a commitment that earned her *Wine Enthusiast*'s 2020 Social Visionary Award. France and its major wine regions have played a starring role in her career evolution, but she holds particular affection for Champagne, where she has led wine tours for groups of travelers since 2016 (including with her boutique wine and wellness travel company À Privé Journeys, which she runs with fellow travel entrepreneur Claire B. Soares). As she puts it, a jaunt to Champagne from Paris is easy and direct, "and makes some of the finest Champagnes, from growers large and small, eminently accessible. What could be better than that?"

Check out Coney's top picks for dining, shopping, and more in Champagne:

Where to stay

If you want to be away from everyone and relax, you stay at the **Royal Champagne**, a thirty-minute drive from Reims. It's luxe, with views overlooking the vines, and has phenomenal food. If you want more of a vibe, you stay in Reims. I tend to book at **La Caserne Chanzy Hotel & Spa**, a Marriott property conveniently located across from the cathedral. Staying here puts you right at the heart of the restaurant and wine bar scene and all the shops and is walkable from the train station. I like knowing that I can go out and head to the wine bars that are open until one A.M. and get back on foot.

Royal Champagne
9, rue de la République, 51160 Champillon

La Caserne Chanzy Hotel & Spa
18, rue Tronsson Ducoudray, 51100 Reims

Where the locals go for coffee and breakfast

The Coffee Champ in Reims
3, galerie d'Erlon, 51100 Reims

This is a specialty coffee bar with pastries and sandwiches. I always make a point of stopping here *after* the hotel breakfast for a little something extra. I generally order the same thing: the croissant aux amandes and a café crème or filter coffee.

For bottle shopping

Les Caves du Forum is a vaulted wine cellar and boutique where I like to go shopping for grower Champagnes and smaller producers. I like supporting the smaller houses when I can because I know their wines are not formulaic. Depending on the day you go, the owner may run an impromptu wine tasting—he opens a bottle and starts pouring as people stand about. It's very relaxed, not a proper or formalized tasting around a table but a great experience.

I also love the **Caves de Sacres**, right across from the hotel, which is practical because they'll deposit the bottles I buy at the hotel. This spot is great for discovering lesser-known producers and accessing very affordable bottles. Given how much more affordable the wines are here, I always come with a wine suitcase.

Les Caves du Forum
10, rue Courmeaux, 51100 Reims

Caves de Sacres
7, place du Cardinal Luçon, 51100 Reims

For lunch

Domaine Les Crayères is an upscale affair that's perfect for a lunch break, which it offers at a more affordable price point. It's even convenient if you're visiting certain Champagne houses nearby. The tasting menu with epic wine pairings may include some Champagne Jacques Selosse—the most innovative, low-yield, and sought-after in the world—if you're lucky. For something more relaxed, head to **Au Bon Manger,** a super small, family-owned cafe and wine shop run by Aline and Eric Serva with a regularly rotating menu (get the house-smoked trout if you see it offered) and a heavy selection of grower Champagnes and natural wines.

Domaine Les Crayères
64, boulevard Henry Vasnier, 51100 Reims

Au Bon Manger
7, rue Courmeaux, 51100 Reims

For an afternoon activity

Once you visit the **Notre-Dame de Reims cathedral**, a UNESCO World Heritage Site, it's time for visits and tastings in the areas around Reims. Uber isn't super reliable outside of the city, so you may want to hire a local taxi (you can even do so upon arrival at the train station) that will stay with you as you visit different Champagne houses. Focus on the villages within thirty minutes of Reims—**Épernay**, **Mareuil-sur-Aÿ**, and **Hautvillers** (this is where Dom Pérignon, who was essential in advancing and pioneering what we now know of Champagne, is buried). You'll get a nice variety of expressions and styles. Book all tastings or visits in advance—it's a popular destination, so you need to plan ahead.

For apéro

I always go to **Le Wine Bar by Le Vintage** to see Nicolas Papavero and his team, who are such champions of local producers. If you can, be there on the fourth Friday of October when the Champenois disgorge bottles right on the street for a sort of boozy block party with sliders and fries to nibble on. You'll also find an oyster pop-up throughout the month of October at the intersection of rue Buirette and rue Jeanne D'Arc. An oyster monger sets up a stall and shucks more than ten different styles of oysters. Everyone eats them and drinks Champagne in the street; it's great fun.

Le Wine Bar by Le Vintage
16, place du Forum, 51100 Reims

For dinner

Gabrielle sits at the foot of the Reims cathedral in a modern building and has a rooftop terrace with the best views of the city and a modern French menu; it's consistently good. Or try **L'Assiette Champenoise** for a Michelin-starred restaurant experience. If you've had your fill of French cooking, head to **Nonna** for Italian—fresh pastas, risottos, and fish. All keep you in the heart of Reims.

Gabrielle
11, rue des Fuseliers, 51100 Reims

L'Assiette Champenoise
40, avenue Paul Vaillant-Couturier, 51430 Tinqueux

Nonna
Parvis de la Cathédrale, 11, rue des Fuseliers, 51100 Reims

TRIP 2: Brittany

by Dominique Crenn & Maria Bello

Dominique Crenn and Maria Bello are no strangers to Paris nor the many worthy destinations accessible within a few hours from the city. Crenn, the French-born avatar of modernist cooking who is the US's most decorated woman chef, may have spent her entire cooking career away from France, but she has always found moments to return to the Breton coast where she spent summers with her parents. Since moving part-time to Paris with Maria Bello, the producer, writer, and Emmy-nominated actress whom she married in 2024, and serving on the jury of *Top Chef France*, the couple has had the opportunity to spend more time in their happy place.

Below, Crenn and Bello share their favorites in this historic part of northwest France:

Where to stay

Villa Tri Men
16, rue du Phare, 29120 Combrit

BELLO: Our go-to is the **Villa Tri Men** in the small port village of Sainte Marine, about twenty minutes by car from Quimper (you can get a direct train from Gare Montparnasse in Paris). It's set up in a maison bourgeoise from 1913 and has sixteen rooms and three cottages, plus a one-Michelin-star restaurant. Villa Tri Men serves the best breakfast, so we always eat there. Plus, you can walk to the beach and all the little restaurants nearby—our favorite, Bistrot du Bac, is located next door.

For lunch

BELLO: We can't visit without lunch at **Crêperie Breizh Izel**, our favorite crêperie. Crêpes and buckwheat galettes originate from this region.
CRENN: Plus, in Locronan specifically, there is a long crêpe tradition. All the ingredients, from the produce to the grains and butter, come from the area. It's the best!
BELLO: Another option in Locronan is **Odette**, which is a more modern restaurant from the owners of the crêperie Ty Coz. The owners have spent a lot of time in San Francisco and have really done something interesting here, something that feels quite Californian. There's a lot of heavy food in the area, but the menu here is lighter—a lot of vegetable soups, salads, and tarts.

Crêperie Breizh Izel
Place de l'Église, 29180 Locronan

Odette
Place de l'Église,
29180 Locronan

For an afternoon snack

Boulangerie le Guillou
Place de l'Église, 29180 Locronan

CRENN: There's only one place to go and that's the **Boulangerie le Guillou** in Locronan, a fifth-generation family-run business. Here, the standouts are two Breton classics, the kouign-amann (a sweet and crispy pastry made from laminated dough and layers of butter with a caramelized finish) and the gâteau breton, which is like a moist shortbread cake.

For shopping

L'Épicerie du Port Sainte Marine
21 rue du Ménez, 29120 Combrit

BELLO: **L'Épicerie du Port Sainte Marine** is a really lovely green grocer where we pick up local produce and cheeses and bring them back to our hotel for picnics when we don't want to go out.
CRENN: They also make their own pâté and have a pâtisserie and prepared foods section. It's among the only shops of its kind in Sainte Marine, and it's very well done.

For afternoon activities

CRENN: Take the time to explore **Locronan** with its incredible Celtic history, granite houses in the Grande Place, and various churches that go back to the fifteenth and sixteenth centuries. The town is so special and feels very untouched. I'd also recommend taking a ferry to the **Glénan Islands**, nicknamed the Breton Tahiti for its white sandy beaches and clear water. There are plenty of places to eat, hike, and partake in water sports.
BELLO: And if time doesn't allow a jaunt over there, use the hotel as a home base and do a more casual coastal hike—something we do on each visit.

For apéro

Le Café de la Cale
3, quai Jacques de Thézac, 29120 Combrit

BELLO: Across the bay from the Villa Tri Men is **Le Café de la Cale**, which is a lovely place overlooking the water to wind down before dinner with cocktails. They also have good charcuterie and cheese platters for nibbling while you drink.

For dinner

Bistrot du Bac
19, rue du Bac, 29120 Combrit

BELLO: We go to the same place every night, the **Bistrot du Bac**.
CRENN: It's run by the same owner as Villa Tri Men, and with the same chef in place for nearly twenty years. They get fresh fish daily, like crab, scallops, and especially langoustine,

directly from Sainte Marine. In fact, the langoustines are why people come to this particular area. It's not farm-to-table, it's *ocean*-to-table. We love it!

TRIP 3: Aix-en-Provence

by Ajiri Aki

Joie de vivre has become something of Ajiri Aki's signature. The author of the book *Joie: A Parisian's Guide to Celebrating the Good Life* and the creator of the lifestyle brand Madame de la Maison, the Nigerian-born entrepreneur has lived out and led retreats with a focus on joy everywhere from the French capital to her second favorite home-away-from-home, Provence. The region—officially called Provence-Alpes-Côte d'Azur—is vast, encompassing six different departments and a stunning diversity of sea and mountainous landscapes. Not all areas are practical for a weekend getaway, but Aki is a big proponent of taking the high-speed train down to Aix-en-Provence, taking in the Impressionist painter Paul Cézanne's birthplace, and driving inland for a solid introduction to the contemporary Provençal way of life.

Read on for Aki's must-visit spots to eat, shop, and explore:

Where to stay

Starting in Aix-en-Provence, there are two great options to serve as a home base: the **Villa Saint-Ange** or **Le Pigonnet**, both occupying eighteenth-century Provençal mansions with lush gardens and pools outside the historic city center. The former really makes you feel like you're staying at someone's private Bastide.

Villa Saint-Ange
7, traverse Saint-Pierre, 13100 Aix-en-Provence

Le Pigonnet
5, avenue du Pigonnet, 13090 Aix-en-Provence

Where to get breakfast

While in Aix, even if you're having breakfast at the hotel, a sweet stop at **Maison Weibel** is a must. The family-run pastry shop and tea salon is known for its calissons (a Provençal confection made from candied fruit and ground almonds), and colombier cake in summer, best enjoyed on the spacious outdoor terrace. There aren't many places for good-quality coffee so naturally, **Mana**, a specialty roaster and brunch café, has become a popular destination.

Maison Weibel
2, rue Chabrier, 13100 Aix-en-Provence

Mana
14, rue Courteissade,
13100 Aix-en-Provence

For a morning activity

I love visiting the open-air "everything" market, which runs three times weekly along the iconic boulevard Cours Mirabeau and stretches down neighboring streets. I go to see the local crafters around the place de Verdun and the five to ten antique vendors set up near the historic Fontaine de la Rotonde. It's a great spot to hunt for antique silver, glassware, and smaller items you can easily cart back on the train.

For lunch

Don't skip out on the restaurants at both of the Aix-en-Provence hotels. Villa Saint-Ange's restaurant **Âma Terra** boasts a menu by Pierre Gagnaire built around local produce, fish, and meat (it's more affordable at lunch). At **La Table du Pigonnet**, the menu is more accessible and the atmosphere in the spectacular garden is great for kids.

Âma Terra
7, traverse Saint-Pierre, 13100 Aix-en-Provence

La Table du Pigonnet
5, avenue du Pigonnet, 13090 Aix-en-Provence

For afternoon activities

The historic center is largely pedestrian, so it's best to walk in from the hotel. Stroll the city center, which is full of gorgeous pastel-hued buildings and tree-lined avenues. For a cultural outing, head to the **Hôtel de Caumont**, an art center housed in an eighteenth-century private mansion with a stunning geometric garden. There are temporary exhibitions (some featuring contemporary artists), a theater that runs a film on the Impressionist painter Paul Cézanne, who was born in the city, and private apartments that you can tour to get a sense of high society living in that era. I recommend sticking around for a cold drink or tea and a pastry in the garden at Café Caumont.

From there, pick up your car and drive twenty minutes to **Château la Coste**, an open-air contemporary art park, wine estate designed by the Pritzker Prize–winning architect Jean Nouvel, and culinary destination. Both Francis Mallman and Hélène Darroze have fine-dining restaurants on-site, and there is also an Italian eatery with pizzas baked in wood-fired ovens, a terrace bistro, and a casual café designed by the Japanese architect Tadao Ando, should you prefer to have lunch here. As you make your way back toward Aix, stop at **Château de la Gaude,** a Relais & Châteaux hotel, restaurant, and wine estate, for a six P.M. group wine tasting, offered daily.

Hôtel de Caumont
3, rue Joseph Cabassol, 13100 Aix-en-Provence

Château la Coste
2750, route de La Cride, 13610
Le Puy-Sainte-Réparade

Château de la Gaude
3959, route des Pinchinats, 13100
Aix-en-Provence

For shopping

In the center of Aix, there's a beautiful retail location for the Provençal brand **Fragonard**. I always go for flowy summer dresses, the occasional antique the shop might display, and fragrances, for which they are most known. I love the citrusy home scent Rêve de Sicile, which the shop sells as a diffuser. For dresses, scarves, or home accessories in Provençal prints, stop by **Souleiado**.

For apéro

Even if you've already had a meal at **Le Pigonnet**, plan to return for a long and leisurely pre-dinner apéritif in the hotel's verdant Mediterranean garden dotted with fountains. If the weather doesn't cooperate, you can stay warm and dry inside at the **1924** bar, which feels like an English club (open October–May).

Le Pigonnet and 1924
5, avenue du Pigonnet, 13090 Aix-en-Provence

For dinner

Gaodina, a quick drive from the city center on the countryside estate of Gaogaïa, is great for outdoor dining during the warmer months. You can also play pétanque, a game akin to bocce ball, and listen to live music while you dine. For lavender seekers, **Terre Ugo** is perfect. From June through August, when this family-owned organic lavender estate is open to the public, the owners run different dining pop-ups. On Thursdays, they set up a cocktail bar and wine bar in the fields and serve homemade tapas. Fridays are picnic-style, with boxes of snacks, wine and beer, and even roasted marshmallows. Book a spot for casual food and, of course, memorable photo ops.

Gaodina
Domaine Gaogaïa, 1075, chemin du Mont Robert, 13290 Aix-en-Provence

Terre Ugo
1885, route du Puy Saint-Réparade, 13540
Aix-en-Provence

Belleville
Buttes Chaumont
Père Lachaise
La Villette

7

h, 20th
SSEMENTS

19th, 20th ARRONDISSEMENTS

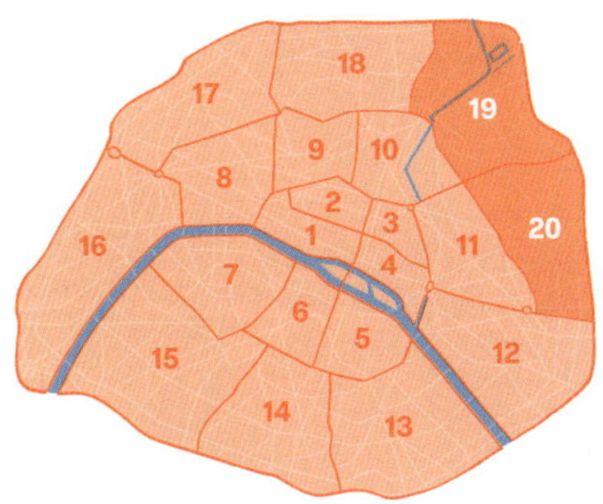

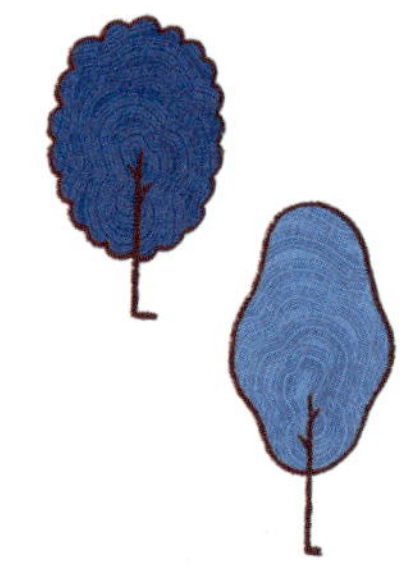

DINING

1. Amagat
2. Ama Siam
3. Bang Bang
4. Le Baratin
5. Buttes Snack Bar
6. Le Cadoret
7. Café de la Musique
8. Cheval d'Or
9. Dandelion
10. Dilia
11. Le Food Market
12. Le Grand Bain
13. Kissproof
14. Lao Siam
15. Mardi
16. Paloma
17. Peppe
18. Les Pères Populaires
19. Sadarnac
20. Soces
21. Yard

SHOPPING

1. Belleville Brûlerie
2. Les Caves de Belleville
3. Drei
4. Le Paon Qui Boit
5. Le Petit Grain
6. Profil Grec

PHILHARMONIE DE PARIS
BD SÉRURIER
RUE MANIN
BUTTES CHAUMONT
RUE DE BELLEVILLE
AVENUE GAMBETTA
BELLEVILLE
20e
RUE BELGRAND
PÈRE LACHAISE
BOULEVARD DE BELLEVILLE
RUE DES PYRÉNÉES
7
15
20
3
8
6
5
6
4
2
14
2
13
16
12
5
3
10
11
1
17
19
21
18
9

19th, 20th ARRONDISSEMENTS DINING

It wouldn't be hyperbolic to call the districts spanning from the Père Lachaise cemetery across and up to Parc de la Villette, one the largest green and cultural spaces in the city, among the most compelling and diverse places to eat and drink in the last decade. With the exception of a few key landmarks like the Père Lachaise, where everyone from Chopin to Jim Morrison earned their final resting place, or the ten-year-old Philharmonie de Paris concert hall designed with spiraling aluminum by Jean Nouvel, these districts have rarely taken up much space on a tourist's itinerary. This historically working-class part of town, with a diverse population from multiple waves of immigration around the hilltop neighborhoods of La Place des Fêtes, Jourdain, and Belleville, is where you'll find the last remaining affordable housing in Paris and destination restaurants like Lao Siam, Le Baratin, and Le Président. They all set up shop in the area decades before it was trending.

By extension, it's also where chefs and food entrepreneurs could find more affordable commercial spaces as rents in central Paris and even gentrifying sections of the 11th arrondissement became prohibitively expensive. As you'll see going north from the cemetery toward the Buttes Chaumont Park and along the Canal de l'Ourcq, these neighborhoods unfold like individual villages because, in reality, they were: the old commune of Belleville and pockets like Ménilmontant and La Villette were annexed to Paris in 1860. You can still find hints of this village vibe in the form of unmarked alleyways dotted with townhouses and picturesque quartiers like Mouzaïa, known for its single-family dwellings with gardens and cobblestone passageways, protected from modern construction due to their location on the fragile subsoil of former gypsum quarries.

More lively are the pedestrian hangouts (pétanque courts aplenty!), cafés, wine bars, and the Paname Brewing Company flanking the Bassin de la Villette, where locals rent electric boats to cruise down the Canal de L'Ourcq, a waterway initiated by Napoleon to bring water into the city, which continues eleven miles outside of the city to Mareuil-sur-Ourcq.

Naturally, each of these areas, some quieter than others, boast their own star indie bakery, under-the-radar restaurant, and specialty bar filled to capacity with locals and a smattering of curious diners and travelers who were well-advised to spend time here, eating, drinking, and exploring beyond the typical haunts.

1. Amagat
23, villa Riberolle, 75020
Up a poorly marked cobblestoned alley flanked by old metalworking ateliers, and off to the left at the end of the passage, is one of Paris's most well-hidden and lively small plates bars. Occupying a former loft, Amagat specializes in Catalan-leaning tapas—marinated lamb chops, ham croquetas, manchego grilled cheese with jalapeño and salsa verde—which clients check off from a printed menu and hand off to their server to place their order. Wash it down with, what else? Spanish natural wines.

2. Ama Siam
49, rue de Belleville, 75019
If big-sister restaurant Lao Siam (located next door) is about restaurant classics, this modern bistro is focused on the Laotian, Vietnamese, Thai, and Chinese recipes the owners grew up eating at home. You could start with the cucumber salad with fermented beans, garlic, and ginger; add on the one-bite miang kham; and split the khao soi, an egg-noodle soup with a curry paste broth topped here with Basque prime rib, as well as the Khao Man Kaï, a variation on the Hainanese chicken rice. Try the Laotian beer or follow the owners' recommendations and opt for a bottle of thoughtfully selected natural wine.

3. Bang Bang
9, rue du Liban, 75020
Whoever said the French can't take heat has evidently never seen the crowds at Bang Bang, Carlos Peñarredonda and Mads Christensen's brightly colored cantina with a menu predicated on spice. Behind a lime-colored counter, the Danish and Colombian chefs prepare small, shareable plates with plenty of kick: fish jelly and chile oysters, sweet and sour sirloin with charred cucumbers, BBQ-marinated chicken on shichimi rice, and for dessert, a grilled plantain split with chai ice cream and coconut crumble, drizzled with dulce de leche.

4. Le Baratin
3, rue Jouye-Rouve, 75020
For thirty years, locals and in-the-know travelers have trekked to the 20th arrondissement for Raquel Carena's cooking at Le Baratin. Run with her partner Philippe Pinoteau, Carena keeps old dishes and techniques alive, like her estouffade de joue de boeuf (smothered beef cheek) and barbajuan (a sort of fried ravioli that originates from the south of France), with unpretentious presentation and a bistro ambiance brought to life by conversation, not music. It's worth going soon—the couple sees retirement on the horizon. Reservations by phone only.

5. Buttes Snack Bar
10, rue Pradier, 75019
If you want to know where the locals go for a casual glass of wine and a smattering of simple small plates, it's this natural wine bar around the corner from the Buttes Chaumont Park, where both the dress code and vibe are laid-back and

the snacks—herring with pickles and spicy sauerkraut, squash maccheroncini with Parmesan and toasted hazelnuts, and juicy pork roast—come on antique dishware.

6. Le Cadoret

1, rue Pradier, 75019

The brother-sister duo Léa and Louis-Marie Fleuriot run this Belleville favorite, known for simple, unfussy, well-executed bistro dishes with a light twist that keep locals coming back time and again. Perched on a corner with unbeatable light a block from the Buttes Chaumont Park, prepare to book (even at lunch) to claim one of the few coveted terrace spots.

7. Café de la Musique

213, avenue Jean Jaurès, 75019

Restaurants in or annexed to museums in Paris have never generated much acclaim, but this sprawling café at the foot of the Cité de la Musique-Philharmonie de Paris concert complex is worth your time, especially if you're exploring the Parc de la Villette or attending a performance. Seasonal bistro staples (scallop risotto, confit lamb shoulder with borlotti beans, or daurade royale) and artisan wines taste all the better when accompanied by live music performances on Fridays and Saturdays, designed to reflect the programming at the Philharmonie and Cité de la Musique.

8. Cheval d'Or

21, rue de la Villette, 75019

As displayed on the façade, Cheval d'Or has been a Chinese restaurant in Belleville since 1987, though it's anything but traditional. Masterfully revived in 2023 by four stars of the wine and food scene, the restaurant is a skillful French-Chinese mashup. Chef Hanz Gueco's menu features creative twists such as leek-vinaigrette salad with seaweed, ginger, and black vinegar; mapo ragu tortellini; a croque-madame with shrimp, fried egg, chile oil and mayo (shown above); and a Sichuan-peppered lamb pithivier (a savory pie made with puff pastry), all served up in a gorgeous space marked by high ceilings, a tone-on-tone gradation of concrete walls, an open kitchen, and Chinese ceramics.

9. Dandelion

46, rue des Vignoles, 75020

If Parisians make a point to come to this leafy square in a quiet section of the 20th arrondissement, it's largely for Dandelion, the first project from Antoine Villard and Morgane Souris. The chef-sommelier team has won over locals with their mid-range and contemporary bistro's approachable elegance (all dark, rough-hewn wood tables, antiqued Italian light fixtures, sheer linen blinds, and ceramic tableware), semi-formal service (they'll clear the crumbs off the table and change your cutlery between courses), and hyper-seasonal menu with broad influences. You'll always find a fresh pasta of some sort, at least two veggie-focused options, memorable fish and meat dishes, like cherry-glazed bonito carefully plated atop Thai chili sauce or guinea fowl prepared two ways, and wildly affordable natural and organic wines by the bottle.

10. Dilia

1, rue d'Eupatoria, 75020

A rustic bistrattoria run by Tuscan chef Michele Farnesi mere feet from the Notre-Dame-de-la-Croix de Ménilmontant church, Dilia is a fresh pasta lover's dream. The menu doesn't stop there—dishes like lobster minestrone, squid in vegetable broth, roasted sea bass with porcini mushrooms, and confit de canard with beetroot take things far beyond Italian cliché. Particularly memorable are the chef's rigatoni alla gricia, paccheri with octopus ragu, and ratatouille ravioli in a Thai broth with guanciale and roasted sesame seeds. Go at lunch for less of a time (and cost) commitment, or dinner for a full tasting experience.

11. Le Food Market

1, boulevard de Belleville, 75020

Since 2015, this pop-up market on the median of the boulevard de Belleville, between the Couronnes and Ménilmontant metro stations, has been a celebration of all manner of international street food. Run on a weekday evening nearly every month (check the website or Instagram for precise programming), and often with thematic focuses, the market has launched Homer lobster rolls, Boneshaker doughnuts, and Nonette bánh mì, and is a platform for top chefs to play with more casual and affordable small-bite dining. Today, with dozens of vendors and a festive vibe, Le Food Market is one of the best introductions to the Parisian street food scene.

12. Le Grand Bain

14, rue Dénoyez, 75020

The epitome of the laid-back, artsy Belleville dining experience can be found at Le Grand Bain, Edouard Lax's small plates and natural wine bar set on a street-art-laden alleyway. Seats are set around a gorgeous central wooden island where guests tuck into gently priced dishes like gougères with lardo di colonnata, their signature panisses (chickpea fritters) dipped in mayo, pork belly with chard and kimchi, or a simple beef tartare that you'll be reluctant to share.

13. Kissproof

50, rue de Belleville, 75020

The Beirut-born bar of the same name switched on its neon sign and opened its yellow doors in Belleville in 2022 and swiftly became the new local favorite and, naturally, is a hit among the Lebanese diaspora. Aside from the stellar cocktail list, organized by style of drink, and the significant selection of both absinthe and riesling, its success can be chalked up to the full food menu. No need to drink and go elsewhere to dine, it's all right here: smoked labneh and stracciatella, a ceviche of daurade royale with puffed corn, lentil salad with diced rutabaga and shanklish cheese, a chipotle-lime chicken sandwich, and a perfect burger.

14. Lao Siam

49, rue de Belleville, 75019

You'll know you've come to the right place when you see the lines forming by 7:30 P.M. to get into this Laotian-Thai institution, located on the rue de Belleville since 1985. Brothers Nicolas, Frédéric, and Alexandre Souksavanh took over the successful operation from their parents in recent years, updating the interiors (now with much better soundproofing) and simplifying the menu with a tighter selection of classic dishes like Laotian sausages served with lemongrass, pan-fried prawns, and the house signature Crying Tiger (a Thai grilled beef dish served with a punchy sauce).

15. Mardi

29, rue de la Villette, 75019

This local favorite coffee shop near the Buttes Chaumont could have followed the pack and limited itself to expertly brewed specialty coffee, a few sweet items, and basic sandwiches. Instead, it elevates the fourth-wave

café format with daily dishes like colorful salads of romanesco broccoli, radicchio, and beetroot-pickled eggs and deconstructed tartines with cumin-roasted vegetables, stracciatella, kumquats, and hazelnuts with a chimichurri sauce. The owners take a similarly broad view of pastry, too, with a display case that covers everything from scones and kanelbullar (Swedish cinnamon buns) to limited edition specials like rhubarb maritozzi, where the brioche is filled with a verbena whipped cream, or strawberry cake with brown butter buttercream.

16. Paloma
93, rue Julien Lacroix, 75020
Eating like a Belleville local means getting a highly coveted seat at Paloma for lunch, where the short fixed menu changes every day. Some days, that's a chicken tourte (pie) with Comté, plated simply on a pool of gravy, others it's white tuna in a rayu (Japanese chile oil) sauce with chickpeas and fennel. Dessert shifts constantly but based on previous hits like chocolate mousse topped with choco-hazelnut crumble, and pets-de-nonne—mini beignets served with a dollop of whipped cream and lemon zest—they'll feel like an end-of-meal hug.

17. Peppe
2, place Saint-Blaise, 75020
At Giuseppe "Peppe" Cutraro's original location of his trio of pizzerias, get a sense of how a charming neighborhood Neapolitan spot turned into a citywide hit. The World Pizza Champion lets his sourdough rise for more than twenty-four hours, bakes it at 734°F (390°C), and it comes out with the soft, puffy edges Neapolitan fans love most. Start with the humble margherita and work your way up to the Queen Tartufo, which mixes local mushrooms, fresh stracciatella, and toasted hazelnuts, with freshly grated truffles from Italy.

18. Les Pères Populaires
46, rue de Buzenval, 75020
A meal at this 20th arrondissement no-frills all-day café is as close as you might get to experiencing Paris like a local. You'll see the regulars who rock up to the bar for an espresso in the morning and a beer at the end of the day, and, in between, those who settle in to lunch on potato salad and zucchini fritters, roasted pork shoulder, and rice pudding on mismatched tables and chairs.

19. Sadarnac
17, rue Saint-Blaise, 75020
In a dining room with whimsical wallpaper and multicolored velvet chairs, chef Lise Deveix serves a surprise tasting menu built around the ingredients she receives daily from small French producers at her modern bistro in the Saint Blaise section of the 20th arrondissement.

20. Soces

32, rue de la Villette, 75019

The quiet intersection of rue de la Villette and rue Fessart has become something of a food lover's hot spot, with Mardi (page 173) lording over one corner and Soces, a sexy seafood-heavy bistro claiming the other. That means you could kick off the afternoon with an excellent coffee and then head across the road for a single oyster with a shot glass–sized margarita (why not?), whelk served simply with mayo, whole grilled mackerel in a bright tandoori sauce, tuna tartare, and for the meat eaters, a sizable pork chop for two. Save room for a particularly good selection of cheese.

21. Yard

6, rue de Mont-Louis, 75011

On the border of the 11th and 20th arrondissements, Yard Cave & Restaurant is textbook eastern Parisian cool. Located on an unexpected village street with restaurants set up in what look like freestanding homes, this spot is kitted out in painted wood, marble, and wrought metal, with a terrace that has the best possible formula for those looking for unfussy, simple dishes (a tarte tatin with leeks and Parmesan; smoked beetroot with ricotta and prunes; roasted sweet potato with miso and peanuts), a plethora of natural wines to choose from, and a lively crowd that spills into the street during the warmer months. Dining aside, it's also a great spot to learn more about natural wine through their Sunday tastings (advanced booking required).

19th, 20th ARRONDISSEMENTS SHOPPING

From the neighborhoods surrounding the Père Lachaise to the village-y pockets of Belleville, Jourdain, and Pyrénées, these districts have their own unique feel and local spirit. A common thread, however, is a strong culture of shopping at specialty stores, various bakeries, and outdoor markets. For well-crafted original goods ranging from coffee to ceramics, start your shopping outing with these standouts.

1. Belleville Brûlerie
14b, rue Lally-Tollendal, 75019
One of the earliest specialty coffee roasters within city limits, Belleville Brûlerie occupies a spectacular, glass-canopied space in a former warehouse. Beans are roasted on-site and available for purchase in the wood-paneled boutique at the front, along with brewed coffees and gear for at-home brewing. Tastings and roastery tours available upon request.

2. Les Caves de Belleville
51, rue de Belleville, 75019
Make a stop at this immense caviste to choose from more than 1,500 biodynamic and natural wines. You can take your bottles to go or enjoy them for on-site apéro with a platter of charcuterie or cheese, but the ideal approach is to sign up for a thematic tasting hosted on Wednesdays and Thursdays—participants get a discount on bottles purchased.

3. Drei
21, rue de la Villette, 75019
From everyday objects for the home to kitchen essentials like glazed stoneware and linen aprons, this Belleville boutique stocks something for everyone. The selection is split between vintage items, like tableware and lighting, and new handcrafted functional pieces made from recycled or compostable materials.

4. Le Paon Qui Boit
61, rue de Meaux, 75019
The zero-proof movement may have been slow to start in France, but it has now found a loyal clientèle thanks to specialty shops like Le Paon Qui Boit (the first of its kind in the country) located between the Canal de l'Ourcq and the Buttes Chaumont Park. On top of a wide range of dealcoholized wines, choose from a host of French-made NoLo spirits and beers, ready-to-drink cocktails, and kombucha.

5. Le Petit Grain
7, rue Dénoyez, 75020
Within eyeshot of its big sister restaurant Le Grand Bain (page 173), Edouard Lax's bakery cranks out hearty sourdough loaves big on complex, nutty flavor; multigrain breads; flavorful focaccia; and classic rye bread alongside a short but original pastry selection of croissants, savory danishes, lamingtons, and peanut tartlets. Unsurprisingly, these breads and tarts are fixtures of the menu down the road.

6. Profil Grec
109, rue de Belleville, 75019
The extra-virgin olive oil that many Parisian chefs swear by can be found at this specialty shop in Belleville, run by Alexandros Rallis since 2009. In addition to the everyday and grand cru olive oil, produced near his mother's native Kalamata in the Peloponnese, you'll find premium cheeses, wine, olives, and bottarga.

BEYOND RESTAURANTS

Bars & Wine Cellars
La Cale
Centre Culturel
Chambre Noire Ménilmontant
Combat
La Commune
Paname Brewing Company
Rosa Bonheur
Supra
Le Toit at La Bellevilloise

Coffee & Tea
Buna Bet
Candle Kids
The Dancing Goat

Pâtisserie, Bread & Ice Cream
Benoit Castel
Boulangerie Milligramme
Ginko Pâtisserie
Parpains

HOW TO GET A SEAT AT THE TABLE

There's a lot that shouldn't be left to chance during a visit to Paris. If you plan ahead and book museum tickets or hire a tour guide months in advance for an afternoon of touring, it only makes sense to think ahead when it comes to dining—especially in one of the most visited destinations in the world. Does every meal need to be mapped out? Of course not. But depending on where you want to dine and whether you have your heart set on any one culinary experience, you'll need to approach mealtime strategically. Here are a few tips to make that a seamless process.

Plan ahead and manage expectations

For some of the most sought-after tables on your wish list, improvising upon arrival or banking on another guest to cancel may lead to disappointment. It's worth going into the planning process knowing which restaurants are painfully challenging, if not entirely impossible, to book, even for locals, and which are realistic with a little bit of effort. Septime (page 108), Frenchie, MoSuke (page 46), Mokonuts (page 106), and Plénitude (a year out at the moment; page 95) are eminently tough. The first two of those restaurants open up their reservations (online only) three weeks in advance, and Mokonuts opens up their bookings two months ahead but fills up quickly. Why is it such a Herculean task? Restaurants and bookable bistros are, for the most part, incredibly compact. It's part of their charm! That's why it's always easier to book a table for two and four than for six or more.

On top of being small, many restaurants have diners that linger, a practice that is unquestionably one of the biggest appeals of drinking and eating in Paris. But it does mean that tables don't turn over very quickly, unless restaurants alert diners when reserving of a time limit. More and more restaurants offer two seatings (deux services), the first at 7 or 7:30 P.M. and the second at 9:30 P.M. or 10 P.M.

Another detail to consider: many restaurants and shops are closed on Sunday and Monday (such as Quinsou, Le Châteaubriand, Kubri, and Passerini; pages 78, 103, 106, and 107, respectively) and some—including popular neo-bistros and fine-dining restaurants such as Comice (page 129), Verjus (page 18), and La Bourse et La Vie (page 13)—are open only during the week.

Book online where possible

Gone are the days when picking up the phone was the only way to get a seat at *any* table. If a restaurant accepts reservations and doesn't stipulate emailing or calling, it is invariably using a provider such as The Fork or Zenchef to manage its bookings, which you'll see directly on the venue's website, social media, or Google listing. To discourage no-shows and last-minute cancellations, restaurants are increasingly using online booking platforms that require a credit-card hold. This will be clear at the time of reserving, and you will receive an automatic email reminding you of the grace period permitted to make any changes or cancellations without being charged.

Still can't get into your dream restaurant, particularly those that accept bookings only by phone, like the Bistrot Paul Bert (page 101)? You'll need perseverance! Better yet, if you are staying in a nice hotel with a concierge, put them to work. And if that fails, heed the advice of Meg Zimbeck, founder of the beloved food tour company Paris By Mouth: "There are so many great restaurants in Paris that it's absurd to stress about the places you can't get into. Just let those go."

Alert the restaurant to any food allergies or intolerances in advance

The good news for travelers with allergies: more and more restaurants in the city, spanning various price points, are able to accommodate or adapt to diners with allergies and food intolerances. Some of the more life-threatening conditions such as Celiac disease or nut allergies may present a challenge they can't meet, but it's important to call or email in advance to discuss with the restaurant whether they can make the necessary adjustments in their kitchens to keep you safe. Just don't show up at the time of your booking and inform the server you're deathly allergic to something or keep a strict vegan diet.

Walk in for a table

Not seeing much availability online? Don't fret yet: Some restaurants choose to limit the number of tables they open up for online booking to leave room for walk-ins, so it may be worth going old school and calling to check the likelihood of getting in that way. You'll want to call shortly before or after lunch or dinner service to reach someone—with the exception of fine-dining establishments or hotel restaurants, Paris restaurants don't employ dedicated hosts or reservationists to answer the phone. You can also show up and hope for the best, but if you do, your best chances for success are at the restaurant's opening or later in the evening, after nine P.M.

Put your name on a waitlist

This isn't a waitlist à l'américaine, where you show up to a restaurant and the host scribbles your name and number onto a piece of paper and calls you in an hour if a table opens up. Instead, you can put yourself on the waitlist ahead of time, either via phone at Mokonuts or online at Le Rigmarole (page 108), Maison (page 106), or La Tour d'Argent (page 47). There are no guarantees you'll get in, but as the French say, ce n'est pas impossible.

Focus on no-reservation spots

The way around the stress of reserving is to focus on establishments that don't accept reservations—and there are plenty! Spacious brasseries like Au Pied de Cochon and Brasserie Dubillot, or wine bars like the chef-in-residence cave à manger Early June (page 104) and L'Avant-Comptoir du Marché (page 75) on the Left Bank, to name but a few, are all fun, delicious, and perfect for those who prefer a touch of dining spontaneity.

PARIS FOOD CALENDAR

Paris and dining go hand in hand on any day of the year, but for those who want a little bit more excitement—or at least, local fanfare—it's worth timing a trip for a number of seasonal events.

JANUARY

Move past the holiday slump with Galette des Rois (Kings' Cake). Every single bakery and pastry shop will offer their take on the frangipane classic for the Epiphany (January 6) and will serve them throughout the month. For more innovative versions and formats, head to pastry shops such as Pierre Hermé, La Maison du Chocolat, Mamiche, Poîlane, Popelini, and more.

END OF JANUARY TO MID-FEBRUARY

Wine Expo & Vinexpo Paris

Producers in wines, spirits, mixed drinks, and low-alcohol, hailing from more than twenty-five countries, come together at this annual fair at the Porte de Versailles convention center to run tastings, master classes, and conferences.

FEBRUARY / MARCH

Salon de l'Agriculture

The annual show at the Porte de Versailles convention center where the French farm, complete with thousands of farm animals, comes to the big city. Somewhat akin to an American state fair, you'll find agricultural professionals, politicians, and the general public hopping between hundreds of stands for tastings and talks.

Le Paris Café Festival

For specialty coffee fans and pros, this annual festival at the Carreau du Temple is the perfect opportunity to discover the country's top shops and roasters.

MAY

Foire de Paris

Since first launching in 1904, this twelve-day fair has been a display of French craftsmanship in everything from textiles and furniture to food and wine. Expect world cuisine and an introduction to French terroir products.

Taste of Paris

The city's premier food festival, featuring outposts from the city's top chefs, restaurants, and specialty food and drink purveyors, inside the glass-canopied nave of the Grand Palais.

JUNE

Fête de la Musique

This is a night full of music timed to the summer equinox. Street concerts accompany special food pop-ups, announced in the weeks prior.

JULY / AUGUST

August is a particularly tricky time to dine due to the number of restaurants that are closed while most Parisians are out of the city on vacation. This is usually a time when hotels and museums will run garden or rooftop food pop-ups and installations (in years past, this included the Cheval Blanc Hotel, the Musée Carnavalet, the Quai Branly Museum, and a block-party setup in front of the Palais de Tokyo, facing the Seine).

SEPTEMBER

Food Temple Festival

This themed street food event brings together established chefs and food upstarts at the Carreau du Temple.

Omnivore Festival at the Parc Floral

A three-day conference featuring hundreds of chefs, producers, bakers, and sommeliers who address the industry's issues du moment.

OCTOBER

Whisky Live Paris and its Cocktail Street at La Villette

The annual tasting and discovery event for whisky amateurs and aficionados organized by La Maison du Whisky.

The Salon du Chocolat

The world's best chocolatiers present their innovations, life-size creations, rare finds, and new releases at Paris Expo Porte de Versailles.

La Fête des Vendanges

The grape harvest festival held in Montmartre (where there are, yes, vines!) since 1934. Food and wine stands are set up at the foot of the Sacré Coeur for tastings.

LATE NOVEMBER TO EARLY DECEMBER

Salon des Vins des Vignerons Indépendants

This annual Independent Winegrowers Wine Fair is held at the gargantuan convention center at Porte de Versailles at the edge of western Paris.

Vini di Vignaioli

The leading wine fair in Paris for Italian artisan winemakers is *the* event of the late fall for natural wine lovers, usually held at the Palais de la Femme.

DECEMBER

It's Bûche time! The city's best pastry chefs roll out their most creative and elegantly decorated Bûches de Noël (yule log cakes) for the end of year festivities. If you find yourself in town in December, this is the confection to taste-test in all of its creative interpretations. You can also book festive teatimes at top hotels (far less costly than a full meal or overnight stay) such as the Ritz Paris, Four Seasons George V, Plaza Athénée, and the Park Hyatt.

WHERE TO EAT NEAR MAJOR TOURIST ATTRACTIONS

Just about any major monument and landmark in Paris is surrounded by a slew of cafés and restaurants, all trying to entice tired visitors to sit down and rest their legs. They are not all created equal, however, so we whittled down the options to a handful of select spots worth your time (and, in some cases, worth reserving in advance).

L'Arc de Triomphe / Champs-Élysées

▸ Le Cinq (page 93)
31, avenue George V, 75008

▸ Le Mermoz (page 131)
16, rue Jean Mermoz, 75008

▸ Restaurant Alan Geaam (page 132)
19, rue Lauriston, 75016

Canal Saint-Martin

▸ Åke (page 101)
8, rue Marie et Louise, 75010

▸ Gros Bao (page 104)
72, quai de Jemmapes, 75010

▸ Holybelly (page 105)
5, rue Lucien Sampaix, 75010

Eiffel Tower

▸ L'Ami Jean (page 75)
27, rue Malar, 75007

▸ Le Jules Verne (page 77)
6, avenue Gustave Eiffel
2nd floor, Eiffel Tower, 75007

▸ Milagro (page 77)
85, avenue Bosquet, 75007

The Louvre

▸ La Halle aux Grains (page 15)
2, rue de Viarmes, 75001
(3rd floor of La Bourse de Commerce)

▸ La Poule au Pot (page 17)
9, rue Vauvilliers, 75001

▸ Yam'Tcha (page 18)
121, rue Saint-Honoré, 75001

The Luxembourg Gardens

▸ Localino (page 77)
10, rue de l'Odéon, 75006

▸ Treize au Jardin (page 86)
5, rue de Médicis, 75006

The Musée d'Orsay

▸ Café des Ministères (page 76)
83, rue de l'Université, 75007

Notre Dame Cathedral

► Chanceux (page 44)
63, rue Galande, 75005

► Shakespeare and Company Café (page 49)
35, rue de la Bûcherie, 75005

► La Tour d'Argent (page 47)
15, quai de la Tournelle, 75005

► Restaurant AT (page 46)
4, bis rue du Cardinal Lemoine, 75005

Palais Garnier

► Espadon (page 94)
15, place Vendôme, 75001

► Galeries Lafayette Gourmet (page 154)
35, boulevard Haussmann, 75009

► Racines (page 17)
8, Passage des Panoramas, 75002

Palais Royal

► 19 Saint Roch (page 12)
19, rue Saint-Roch, 75001

► Juveniles (page 15)
47, rue de Richelieu, 75001

► Kunitoraya (page 15)
1, rue Villedo, 75001

► Verjus (page 18)
52, rue de Richelieu, 75001

Panthéon

► Kitchen Ter(re) (page 45)
26, boulevard Saint-Germain, 75005

► Kokoro (page 45)
36, rue des Boulangers, 75005

► Otto (page 46)
5, rue Mouffetard, 75005

Père Lachaise

► Amagat (page 171)
23, villa Riberolle, 75020

► Dandelion (page 172)
46, rue des Vignoles, 75020

► Sadarnac (page 174)
17, rue Saint-Blaise, 75020

Place de la Bastille

► Bistrot des Tournelles (page 12)
6, rue des Tournelles, 75004

► Mokonuts / Mokoloco (page 106)
5, rue Saint-Bernard, 75011
74, rue de Charonne, 75011

► La Sabicherie (page 88)
33, rue du Faubourg Saint-Antoine, 75011

► Taverna (page 108)
56, rue Amelot, 75011

Sacré Coeur

► a.léa (page 149)
39, rue Lamarck, 75018

► Le Maquis (page 151)
53, rue de Cloÿs, 75018

► Mehmet (page 151)
43, rue Ramey, 75018

► Sushi Shunei (page 152)
3, rue Audran, 75018

Trocadéro

► Comice (page 129)
31, avenue de Versailles, 75016

► Les Marches (page 131)
5, rue de la Manutention, 75016

► Substance (page 132)
18, rue de Chaillot, 75016

ACKNOWLEDGMENTS

FROM THE AUTHOR

Writing about gastronomy and Paris, in all of their evolutions, is a joy that I have been fortunate to pursue for much of my career. But that delight cannot be disconnected from the people who have given me opportunities to research and document my favorite city on earth; people such as Stephanie Wu and Lesley Suter of Eater who have assigned me many stories over the years; Laura Dozier, my longtime editor at Abrams; and the best champion I could ask for, Judy Linden. Thank you all for bringing me on board for this exciting project. To my husband, Cédric, and dear friends who accompanied me to many taste-testing meals, je vous remercie—your trained palates and keen observations were invaluable. A huge thanks to Sara Lieberman and Brent Longley for their support along the way and, of course, to Parisians of all backgrounds, inspirations, visions, and tastes, without whom my work would not be possible. Merci!

FROM THE EDITOR

Thank you first and foremost to Lindsey Tramuta, a longtime Eater contributor who has helped travelers navigate Paris's restaurant scene for so many years—this book would not be what it is without your dedication, thoroughness, and enthusiasm for dining out repeatedly in the name of journalism.

Thank you to Britt Aboutaleb, Amanda Kludt, and Eric Karp for bringing this idea to life, and to Ellie Krupnick for keeping us on track. Thank you to Lesley Suter for your help conceptualizing this book and being a voice of reason and calm through the many edits. Thank you to Hilary Sharp, the MVP who steered the project and made this book happen with an unflappable ability to get things done. Thank you to Alice Des for the way you've brought the city to life through illustrations, to Nat Belkov and Lille Allen for the design vision, and to Hannah Steinkopf-Frank for fact-checking. Thank you to Aude White and Dane McMillan for making sure people know about everything we do.

Thank you to Laura Dozier, Diane Shaw, and Jenice Kim at Abrams for being our ever-patient partners through this massive project. Thank you to Annalea Manalili and Amy Treadwell for your careful reads. Thank you to Natasha Martin, Mamie Sanders, and Danielle Kolodkin at Abrams for their enthusiastic publicity and marketing efforts.

Finally, thank you forever to the writers, editors, reporters, illustrators, and designers at Eater, many of whom love Paris as much as they love their home cities, for always championing coverage of Paris and its food culture in any shape and form.

INDEX

Page references in *italics* refer to illustrations.

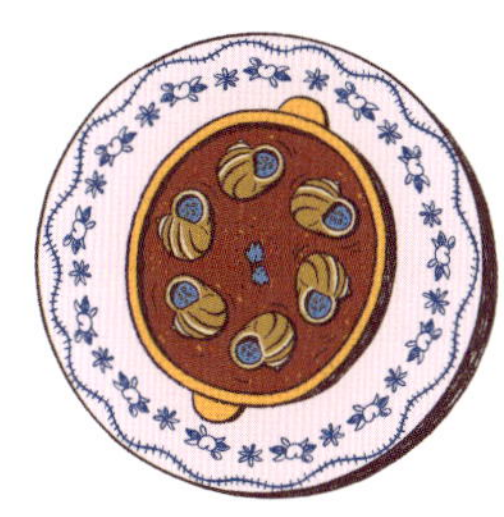

D

E

F

G

H

I

J

K

L

M

N

O

P

Editor: Laura Dozier
Designer: Jenice Kim
Managing Editors: Annalea Manalili and Lisa Silverman
Production Manager: Larry Pekarek

Library of Congress Control Number: 2024942514

ISBN: 978-1-4197-6584-1
eISBN: 978-1-64700-892-5

Printed and bound in China
10 9 8 7 6 5 4 3 2 1

ABRAMS The Art of Books
195 Broadway, New York, NY 10007
abramsbooks.com

Look for other guides in the series, including those to New York City, Los Angeles, and Mexico City.

EATER is a digital media brand dedicated to all things food and dining. The Eater network comprises a national site covering restaurants, cooking, and food culture, more than twenty city sites tracking local dining scenes, a robust YouTube channel featuring documentary-style videos about the inner workings of restaurants, and a variety of social channels, all run by a diverse team of writers, editors, producers, and contributors. Eater has been recognized by numerous awards organizations for its achievements in food journalism and media, including the James Beard Awards, the American Society of Magazine Editors, and the New York Emmys.

Lindsey Tramuta is a French American journalist and author based in Paris since 2006. She is a regular contributor to the *New York Times*, Eater, *Condé Nast Traveler*, *Bloomberg*, and other international publications, in which she covers the intersection of culture, travel, and business. Her first book, *The New Paris: The People, Places & Ideas Fueling a Movement*, looks at the evolving French capital while her second, *The New Parisienne: The Women & Ideas Shaping Paris*, deconstructs the myth of the Parisian woman and showcases more than forty women influencing Paris. *The New Paris*, an interview podcast Tramuta has hosted since 2017, is the continuation of both projects.

Alice Des is a French artist and illustrator from the North of France who is now based in Paris. After four years as an illustrators' agent, she decided to become a freelance artist herself, working with different media and techniques. She has collaborated with global brands including the *Washington Post*, *Die Zeit*, *Les Echos*, Adobe, Eurostar, Lillet, Petrossian, and more. You can find her work at Slow Galerie in Paris.

17e
8e
16e
7e
15e
14e